LIVING IN THE KEY OF JOY

Volume V

Stories to inspire you to strengthen your faith, deepen your connections, and release more joy

PRESENTED BY GAIL CLANTON

FOREWORD BY ANDREA T. MARTIN

Cover design by Janet Harward, JanetDesign

Janetharward.myportfolio.com

ISBN 979-8-9880242-1-7

LIVING IN THE KEY OF

JOY

Stories to inspire you
to strengthen your faith,
deepen your connections,
and release more joy

Presented by Gail Clanton
Clanton Communications, LLC

DEDICATION

The first volume of *Living in the Key of Joy* was published in 2021, featuring inspiring stories from twenty remarkable women. Unfortunately, four of these women have passed away.

This fifth and final volume is dedicated to their memory:

Diane Ables

Suzanne L. Anderson

LaVonne Dees

Carol Johnson

I will be forever grateful for their courage and willingness to share their stories with me, a first-time anthology presenter.

May their souls continue to rest in peace.

TABLE OF CONTENTS

Foreword
By Andrea T. Martin

Sarah said, "God has brought me laughter,
and everyone who hears about this
will laugh with me." Genesis 21:6

Oh how this Scripture resonates with me today. Let me explain…

When Gail Clanton, the presenter of this amazing collection of stories, approached me about writing the Foreword for this book I was elated. I've known Gail for many years, in fact we first met when she was a client of mine. I have respected the work she's poured into these *Living In The Key of Joy* anthologies and was honored to be invited to be a part of her labor of love. So, when she asked, I didn't hesitate to give her a heartfelt "yes." And then life happened.

Shortly thereafter, I was diagnosed with breast cancer. Breast cancer. Me, the Motivational Speaker, International Author, and Christian Life Coach. Me, the Bank Executive who was just about to leave the country to work abroad. And, me, the woman who had just obligated herself to write about joy.

Really? Joy? How in the world was I going to write about joy when I was going through one of the most difficult chapters of my life? Honestly, joy was one of the furthest things from my mind. But then I thought about Sarah.

The Bible tells us that Sarah was a woman of advanced age, yet God had promised her husband that she would bear him a child. I can only imagine Sarah's doubt. In today's terms, Sarah was menopausal! How was she going to fulfill the dreams of her husband and the will of God? It just didn't seem practical. As the story goes on, we are reminded that God's promises are true, and Sarah does bear Abraham a son who is named Issac. When this happened, Sarah laughed! Genesis 21:6 states, "God has brought me laughter, and everyone who hears about this will laugh with me."

Now let me step back for just a moment. As I mentioned earlier, the promise of God probably didn't seem practical to Sarah. This speaks to me, and it may speak to you, too. Sometimes our current situations seem dreary and the promise of good health…or the promise of financial security…or the promise of better relationships…or the promise of JOY, can seem impractical. You may find yourself asking God, "Father, how can I dare to hope for good things while I sit in the middle of pain and chaos?"

That's where our faith comes into play. We can experience joy in the midst of our troubles. That's just one of the many benefits of having a relationship with God. We have the supernatural ability to smile in the midst of pain and to laugh when nothing around us seems or feels funny.

So as I write this today, I have joy. I don't feel my best, I don't look my best, but I'm enjoying the laughter around me as I anticipate more joyous days ahead.

How about you?

If you're in the midst of a troubling time, I encourage you to dig deep and find the joy that resides within you. Joy is an inside job, you can CHOOSE joy. It's a powerful weapon against fear and negative thoughts. Use it to your advantage and watch your world change for the better.

The Word of God tells us that the joy of the Lord is our strength! I encourage you, as I encourage myself, to trust, believe, and embrace joy in every way possible.

And if you've just come out of a storm, I hope you're laughing and experiencing the joy of victory! I hope you're rejoicing as you think of how life thought it had beaten you down, yet you've rebounded and can tell your story – just as others have shared their stories in the pages that follow.

As you begin this book, I ask you to consider these three tips for laughing and finding joy, no matter what life looks like:

J – Be JUBILANT. In the book of Psalms, God tells the fields to be jubilant and for the trees to sing for joy. I suggest that you do the same.

O – Remain OPTIMISTIC. Have you ever thought about how hard the caterpillar has to struggle to release itself from the chrysalis and to become a beautiful butterfly? The fight was tough, but the caterpillar believed it could do what was needed and knew that the fight would be worth it. That same fight, determination and optimism resides within you. Don't forget to use it.

Y – Say YES. Dream big, plan for success, and believe that anything is possible. Say "yes" to God's will in your life and let Him be your guide.

Now I better understand God's timing. I needed to write this Foreword now because, as I sit through this difficult time in my life, I am encouraged by my own words. I hope I've encouraged you, too. Together we can learn the lessons, share our stories, and feel the joy – no matter what.

JOY Disguised

By Gail Clanton
Project Presenter

JOY Disguised

By Gail Clanton

As the creator of the *Living In The Key of Joy* anthology series, I've had stories included in each of our previous volumes. I've shared details of joyous experiences and relationships, and I've usually had a fairly easy time deciding what to write. But not this time. This time I've struggled a bit.

Maybe it's because I realize that this is the fifth and final volume. Maybe it's because life has been very interesting this past year. And maybe, just maybe it's because I've come to the conclusion that joy can be quite elusive. Joy doesn't always look or feel like joy.

Joy comes in all shapes, forms, and sizes. And what looks like joy to one person may look like something totally different to the next person.

Joy is often disguised, masked to look like something other than what it is. To more clearly illustrate my point, I'll share seven personal examples from my own book of life:

Joy disguised as a scream. I don't often visibly lose control, but on that day I did. I was tired, upset, and I'd just about had enough.

I'd started the day in a morning meeting at work where a new policy was presented. The policy made no sense to me. It was so ridiculous, so I thought, that it made me question why I worked for a company that would propose such madness. But then I remembered my mortgage and other bills and soon the answer to that question became very clear. I had bills to pay.

The balance of the workday was met with one question after another, so much so that I wanted to put my head down on the desk and wait for someone to bring me milk and cookies. It was also met with a phone call from a guy I'd met and wished I hadn't. Dag. Where was that silver spoon when I needed it?

Finally, the workday was ending, and I was so happy to be meeting a friend downtown to see a play. But then I got lost going to the theater. Another friend was on the phone trying to help me with directions but, truth be told, just the sound of his voice was irritating at that point. I tell you, I'd had enough.

You see, I was in the middle of a difficult divorce and it didn't take much to get on my nerves in those days. The combination of the workday mess and the confusion of the evening rush hour was simply more than I could take.

So I screamed.

I screamed at the traffic, at my life, and I screamed at God. I could not understand why He couldn't give me a break! Wasn't I already going through enough? Why did I now have to adhere to dumb office rules and why did I have to be lost in rush hour traffic?

Once I got over myself, I felt a calm that I hadn't felt in a long time. Maybe I just had to let that frustration out. I apologized for screaming at God and I know He forgave me because I soon found my way to the theater and I had a wonderful evening.

That scream provided me with a much-needed release. And that felt like joy.

Joy disguised as a watermelon. I have many fond memories of my father, and one of them revolves around our shared love of watermelon. I remember going with him to pick them out and then cutting the watermelon in our kitchen, hoping that we'd been lucky enough to get a sweet one. I remember clearly how he'd cut the watermelon in half and then take a thin slice off the top of one of the halves. That slice was the "tester".

I continue to enjoy a good watermelon and I slice it, just like I did with my father. And then I cut that thin slice off the top. But now I bite into it and then I raise it up to the ceiling (heaven) and smile. That's my way of saying, Daddy, I think we got a good one!" For me, in that moment, that watermelon feels like joy.

Joy disguised a trip to the mall. If you were to check the dictionary for "shopaholic" you would find my picture, along with a few of my closest friends. I love to shop and I love to hang out with people who love to shop. Whether we're going to a local shopping center… taking a road trip to an outlet mall… enjoying a bus trip… or shopping in another country, shopping has got to be one of my most favorite things to do.

It's the camaraderie, the laughs, the conversation, just fun of it all that I enjoy. For me, shopping feels like joy.

Joy disguised as a kitchen table. Back in the "old days" when I was growing up, families often ate together at a table in the kitchen. My family was no exception.

I remember the meals my mother lovingly prepared for the family, and I remember the conversations we had at that table. The years have passed, but that green formica table is still standing. In more recent times, the table serves as the gathering place for my weekly coffee dates with my mother and fun talks with other family members and friends. It's still doing its job of giving us a gathering place to share, to remember, and to love. That feels like joy.

Joy disguised as a cat. Now hear me out. I am fully aware of the fact that a lot of people don't like cats. They frown upon their peculiarities and their attitudes. They don't understand how we can feed them and love them, yet the cat will not come when we call them and will stare us down in a mean, menacing way if we challenge them. They struggle to comprehend how cats pay no bills yet rule the house. I get it. But these are the exact things I love about cats. Unlike dogs, cats make you earn their affection and doing so isn't always easy.

I've had cats in my life for as long as I can remember, so I know them well. I also know that my current cat, Sasha Malia is one of the best.

She's crazy and quirky, and she's all mine. Sasha Malia feels like joy.

Joy disguised as a restless night. I remember one night I just couldn't sleep. I was dealing with a troubling situation and couldn't figure out what should be my next move. So, in the midst of my ongoing, yet fruitless, internal deliberations, I tossed and turned and turned and tossed for much of the night. It was bad.

Then, at some point around 2am, I was reminded of my faith. And I remembered that I had access to a God who already knew the answers I was struggling to find. So I got out of bed, with tears of frustration in my eyes, and literally bounced an invisible basketball up to God. It was my way of saying, "God, you got next. I know you can handle this because I know that I can't. I'm done. It's in your hands now."

Was the problem solved? Nope. Did I feel better? Heck yeah! Because I knew that I finally surrendered to someone much more powerful than me. I knew I had someone who would bear my load. And, eventually, that restless night felt like joy.

Joy disguised as mango smoothie. I've been divorced for about 14 years and the living alone lifestyle isn't exactly for me. Sure, I enjoy my independence and solitude, but I have also missed having a special person who can make this thing called life more fun and interesting.

In the fall of last year, I took a chance and met a man at a local food court. It was an interview of sorts, we were feeling each other out, trying to decide if there was any potential there for a meaningful relationship.

We met late morning, so for me, it was a little too late for coffee and too early for lunch. So I ordered a mango smoothie.

That smoothie gave me the opportunity to meet a really nice guy! We talked and laughed and shared and made plans to see each other again soon. And guess what? He's still in my life and we're still talking and laughing and sharing and making plans. That mango smoothie felt like joy.

There you have it! Seven examples of joy disguised as:

1. A scream
2. A watermelon
3. A shopping trip
4. A kitchen table
5. A cat
6. A restless night
7. A mango smoothie

It was important to me to include seven examples because, Biblically speaking, seven is the number representing completion. This final volume of *Living In The Key of Joy* represents a job completed.

My life has been made richer because of this project and the women and men who have been a part of it. I extend a special shout-out of thanks to Dr. Katrina Miller and Yolanda Gail Fields-Witherspoon who have participated in each of the five volumes. I also thank my brother, George Clanton, for his constant help and support throughout the JOY journey.

My wish for all of the authors is that they each continue to be happy, stay well, and live their lives in the amazing Key of Joy. I wish the same for you, dear reader.

Now buckle up and prepare to enjoy these amazing and uniquely written expressions of joy. I hope you will enjoy them and use them as a catalyst to recognize, appreciate, and embrace the joy that surrounds you.

The JOY of Hearing God's Voice

By Selece W. Bowman

The JOY of Hearing God's Voice

By Selece W. Bowman

My ability to hear God's voice has been a process. I would like to share a few meaningful moments I've experienced while traveling this path, focusing on 1) how it started, 2) worship, 3) soaking prayer, 4) a desire to hear, and 5) distractions.

1. How it started

I can clearly recall the first time I heard the voice of God. I was in my senior year of high school. As I was praying and asking God for guidance to make the right choices for my future, I read in Jeremiah 29:11, "for I know the plans I have for you, declares the Lord, plans for welfare and not for evil, to give you a future and a hope." I believed that God was in control of my future and had good plans for me. Soon I noticed my worries lessened, as I held on to these words, and read that verse regularly. (I continue to read it even to this day.) As I was praying and asking God to please make things clear, I also asked Him not to let me doubt that what I heard was coming from Him. This is because I was beginning to question God about what I was hearing on some days. I can remember thinking, "Oh, I hope this is from God, and not the enemy in disguise."

As I was nearing the date for my high school graduation, and as I was receiving college acceptance letters, I pondered which school to attend. While trying to make my decision, I heard a voice say, "stay home." I immediately realized that I had not considered applying to any colleges near my hometown, even though there were many excellent schools in the Washington, DC area. I had plans to leave town, so I never thought about any of them. Soon thereafter, I caught the bus to Howard University and submitted my application. I believed that was God's voice I heard directing me to stay home and to apply to Howard right away, because the day I went to the admissions office was the last day they were accepting applications. I was asking myself, "why had I not applied to Howard University earlier?" I had even worked at Howard one summer in the Upward Bound program and thoroughly enjoyed the experience of being on a campus where so much history had been made. But my thought at the time was to go to school away from home. I never regretted staying home, especially knowing that God had directed me to do so.

When I looked back on it, I was not ready to leave the support system of my mother and sister. My father had passed away when I was almost 16 years old, which was the summer before I entered high school. My father, mother, sister and I were very close and, when dad died, the three of us grew closer. Of course, I prayed about it and when I received my acceptance letter from Howard, I felt at peace with the decision. I met my future husband (a native Washingtonian, too), while attending Howard and I made some lifelong friends, people I've kept in touch with for over 40 years. When the time came to go to graduate school, I made plans to leave town, but that didn't happen either. My graduate studies were also completed in Washington, DC.

As I said earlier, this was about the time I started to really pray and wait to hear God's answers. I also started to journal daily. I was clearly hearing God give me directions and I wanted to write them down. I wanted to be able to go back and read them.

To this day, I read my daily devotions and Scriptures. I often receive a message in my heart and ears. Sometimes, it's in my thoughts and other times, I can clearly hear a voice speaking. It is always a soft voice, one that requires that I am quiet in order to hear it. I think of Psalms 46:10, "Be still and know that I am God." Over the years, I have learned to sit still and wait on God. It has not always been easy, but now it comes naturally. We have a tendency to go to God asking in prayer, and although He does tell us to ask, we talk and ask some more, forgetting to just spend quiet time with God.

Quiet time allows us to hear God speak, however His voice may sound to you. After hearing from God, I ask, "Was that for me or others?" I wait to receive my answer, and then I act. If it is for others, I often share the Scripture and what God gave me on my Facebook page. Many people have told me that they are very encouraged by those posts. If it is for someone specifically, I reach out to that person. There have been times when I have a random encounter with someone, and I am given the opportunity to share the word I received from God that morning. I love when God divinely sets up such an encounter.

While serving with my husband as prayer coordinators at my church, I often asked people before praying for them to open their ears to hear what God wants to tell them. Prior to this, while preparing for altar ministry, I would ask God to give me a clear word for those I pray for. On occasion, there would be someone praying louder than me and I would hear God say "Tell them to just listen." At that moment, I often felt the atmosphere shift, and I'd watch that person settle their spirit and receive the word from God. Before they left the altar, I would ask them if they spent time just waiting to hear from God when they prayed. Then I would encourage them to not just pray asking or thanking God, but to also find time to sit quietly and begin to recognize how they specifically hear from Him. Some of the ways we can hear God are through dreams, words, pictures, and music. God often speaks to me through music. I can hear a song and get so encouraged, uplifted, motivated, and just Blessed.

I love to caption this time as "From God's mouth, to my ears." These are such special moments, and they have carried me through some extremely difficult times in my life. I feel joyful when I hear God's voice.

2. Worship

Worship takes me to a place I want and need to be. It draws me very close to God. I encourage others to use worship music, especially if they find it hard to sit quietly, while waiting to hear from God. A favorite song of mine is "There is None like You." The lyrics are:

I worship you, oh mighty God,
There is none like you,
I worship you, oh prince of peace,
That is what I long to do.
I give you praise,
for you are my righteousness,
I worship you oh mighty God,
There is none like you.

This is one of my favorite songs to sing. It helps me center myself, clear my mind and just focus on God.

3. Soaking Prayer

At my church, we have a time set aside for soaking prayer. Soaking prayer is a type of Christian prayer that involves resting in God's love and presence. It is a time to truly relax and pray for an extended period of time, while keeping your mind free of other thoughts. Believe it or not, it is not easy for many people to do. I have met people who have said they could not shut their minds down to just focus during soaking prayer. I suggested they make time for soaking at home, in short periods of time. If they fall asleep, they are at home and can continue resting, wake up and even soak some more.

I love to engage in soaking prayer at home, and often afterwards my mind feels so clear and focused on the music and I am ready to hear from God. As I end my prayer, I get a pen and paper because I know God is going to talk to me and I want to be ready to hear Him and get all He has for me. It is just an amazing and refreshing time. I encourage you to try this type of prayer to help you begin to focus yourself, clear your mind and possibly hear the voice of God. It takes some practice, but it will truly bring you joy!

4. A Desire to Hear

While home recuperating from surgery in 2011, I had numerous concerns, so I decided to take that time to sit quietly before God. I wanted to position myself to hear from Him. That was my heart's desire. I truly wanted to hear what God had to say about my health, my family, my job, my business and everything else. I had already followed His instructions from 1 Peter 5:7, "Casting all your care upon him, for he careth for you." This was easy for me, because when I was growing up, my mother used to tell me, anything that concerns you, concerns God. So, daily during this time, I prayed, read Scriptures and waited to hear from God. I was in a state of expectancy and on the third day, God spoke to me about many things. He was very specific and reminded me to write things down. Of course, I had my pen and paper, ready to journal.

At first, I was surprised by how clear His instructions were. Then, I recalled how I asked Him many years before to make things clear to me and not let me doubt if the instruction I was receiving was from Him. As

I wrote in "Living In The Key of Joy, Volume 3", this was a time of trusting God and this was when my faith increased tremendously. At the time, I followed His instructions to resign from my job and start my business. I thought I was going in one direction, and He took me in a completely different direction. I had used up numerous pens and written in several tablets by the end of my recuperation period. I was in awe of God. Just reading all the things He said to me amazed me so much. One day, I will write a book about it.

5. Distractions

Be aware of your distractions. We are so busy today. Most of us have so much going on, and often there is no down time. Many people have no time for God in their schedule. I encourage you to make time in your schedule to hear from God. The enemy has conjured up all types of distractions; things to keep us busy and then he even makes us believe that we cannot live without those things. I completely understand, times are changing and we need to have access to all this technology that exists today. But I also urge you to recognize what keeps you so busy and, if you can, dial it back, put it down or pull away from it. Make these changes to help you center yourself and focus on hearing the voice of God.

I also encourage you to begin to establish or modify your quiet time. Answering the following questions will help you:

1. Do you have a personal relationship with God?
2. Have you ever heard a sermon and knew that the preacher was speaking directly to you from God?
3. How do you hear from God? (Dreams, words, pictures, music?)
4. How often do you sit before God and just listen?
5. Can you find more time in your day to spend with God?

In conclusion, I want you to think of what God has revealed to you through your prayer time. Spend some time thinking about God's faithfulness. How has He provided for you in the past? How is He providing for you right now? Stay in the same perspective and begin talking to Him about your concerns.

Ask God to continue to be the focus of your life and to make His presence known to you. Ask God to draw you closer to Him, so you can know Him deeper and experience the joy that only He can provide. Thank God for His grace and mercy He has bestowed upon you.

Then wait to hear His voice!!

In the Midst of Adversities, Count It All JOY

By Dr. Jamie J. Brown, D.Hum., CPLC

In the Midst of Adversities, Count It All JOY

By Dr. Jamie J. Brown, D.Hum., CPLC

Please take a moment to clear your mind and your surroundings. Allow yourself to be fully present in the current moment as you prepare to read this chapter. Remove any distractions that may prevent you from receiving a word of encouragement or inspiration. Feel free to get your preferred beverage, your journal, your favorite writing instrument, whether it be a pen or pencil, and settle into your favorite corner or space; you may even light a candle if you so choose.

As mentioned in the Bible, "count it all joy" serves as our primary focus throughout this chapter. I invite you to engage in a contemplative exercise by meditating and journaling on the various versions of this text. As you read each Scripture, I encourage you to reflect on which one resonates most deeply with you and identify any specific aspects that stand out.

James 1:2-4 NKJV (New King James Version)

“My brethren, count it all joy when you fall into various trials, knowing that the testing of your faith produces patience. But let patience have its perfect work, that you may be perfect and complete, lacking nothing.”

James 1:2-4 TPT (The Passion Translation)

"My fellow believers, when it seems as though you are facing nothing but difficulties, see it as an invaluable opportunity to experience the greatest joy that you can! For you know that when your faith is tested it stirs up in you the power of endurance. And then as your endurance grows even stronger, it will release perfection into every part of your being until there is nothing missing and nothing lacking."

James 1:2-4 MSG (The Message Translation)

"Consider it a sheer gift, friends, when tests and challenges come at you from all sides. You know that under pressure, your faith-life is forced into the open and shows its true colors. So don't try to get out of anything prematurely. Let it do its work so you become mature and well-developed, not deficient in any way."

James 1:2-4 NLT (New Living Translation)

"Dear brothers and sisters, when troubles of any kind come your way, consider it an opportunity for great joy. For you know that when your faith is tested, your endurance has a chance to grow. So let it grow, for when your endurance is fully developed, you will be perfect and complete, needing nothing."

Which Scripture resonated with you and why? (Journal it.)

As I begin this chapter, I gently remind you to take a moment to breathe and extend grace to yourself, acknowledging that all is well. Perhaps you may also benefit from a brief pause, allowing yourself the opportunity to breathe and simply be present. Regardless of your current circumstances, I invite you to take several deep breaths. As you exhale, release any negative thoughts, uncertainties, or obstacles that may be holding you back. Inhale positivity and uplifting thoughts, focusing on what brings you certainty. Take a deep breath and release it.

How do you feel at this moment? (Journal it.)

Inhale & Exhale.

Let's dive into our reading. The Bible says in James 1:2-4 NKJV, "My brethren, count it all joy when you fall into various trials, knowing that the testing of your faith produces patience. But let patience have its perfect work, that you may be perfect and complete, lacking nothing."

I've endured many trials and tribulations in my life, from grief of losing my loved ones, job loss, a toxic relationship, an eviction notice, domestic violence, molestation, financial challenges, health challenges, miscarriage, bullying, barriers due to my disability (deafness), lack of accessibility, body shaming, mental and emotional abuse from a narcissistic relationship, and the absence of a sense of belonging.

Every experience one encounters serves as an opportunity for learning and personal growth. It is crucial to reflect on these experiences and discern the valuable lessons they hold. As a life coach, I often pose the following questions to my clients: "What can be learned from this experience? What insights does it offer at this moment?" I have also found it beneficial to ask myself these same questions.

Life presents various challenges and difficulties that can either make us bitter or better. The trials and tribulations we experience are not meant to harm us but to strengthen our faith and trust in God. The Bible says in Proverbs 3:5-6 NKJV, "Trust in the Lord with all your heart; And lean not on your own understanding; In all your ways acknowledge Him, And He shall direct your paths." He also stated in Jeremiah 29:11 NKJV, "For I know the thoughts that I think toward you, says the Lord, thoughts of peace and not of evil, to give you a future and a hope."

In his book "Christian Counseling," Gary R. Collins, Ph.D. stated: "Grief is a normal response to the loss of any significant person, object, or opportunity. It is an experience of deprivation and anxiety that can show itself in one's behavior, emotions, thinking, physiology, interpersonal relationships, and spirituality. Grief is not limited to the loss of a loved one through death. Any loss can bring grief, including divorce, retirement from a job, amputation of a limb, the departure of a child to college or a pastor to some other church, moving from a friendly neighborhood (or watching a good neighbor move), losing a home or other valued possession, the death of a pet or plant, loss of a contest or athletic game, health failures, or even the loss of one's youthful appearance, confidence, or enthusiasm. Sometimes, desirable and long-anticipated events—like the move to a better job or graduation from college—can bring grief (mixed with happiness) because valuable memories or relationships are being lost and left behind. Doubts about one's faith, the waning of spiritual vitality, or disillusionment about the actions of a trusted religious leader can all lead to sadness and emptiness that indicate grief. In summary, whenever a part of life is lost or taken away, there can be grief."[1]

I've had my own unique experiences with grief and loss. I lost my father and sister within a nine-month span of time. Furthermore, both of my grandparents passed away while I held their hands. Those two events, which happened several years apart, were especially difficult periods in my life. When I was approximately 19 years of age, I had my initial experience as a caregiver. It was during these challenging times that I discovered my inner strength and resilience.

[1] Gary R. Collins, *Christian Counseling 3rd Edition: Revised and Updated - A Comprehensive Guide* (reprint ed., Thomas Nelson, 1988), 992 pages.

Let me share a personal story with you…

It was a Friday morning, and I was getting ready to go to work. The night before, I had a dream that made me wake up sweating profusely. In my dream, God spoke to me very clearly, telling me not to leave the house after I returned home from work that evening. I was to stay at home. Although I did not understand the reason behind this instruction, I decided to follow God's command.

I attended work and felt a sense of unease throughout the day. My concentration was affected, and I was deeply troubled by that dream. I found myself shedding tears uncontrollably. In an effort to regain my composure, I reminded myself to remain calm and recited the 23rd Psalm.

Psalms 23:1-6 NKJV

"The Lord is my shepherd; I shall not want. He makes me to lie down in green pastures; He leads me beside the still waters. He restores my soul; He leads me in the paths of righteousness For His name's sake. Yea, though I walk through the valley of the shadow of death, I will fear no evil; For You are with me; Your rod and Your staff, they comfort me. You prepare a table before me in the presence of my enemies; You anoint my head with oil; My cup runs over. Surely goodness and mercy shall follow me All the days of my life; And I will dwell in the house of the Lord Forever. Amen."

As I recited the psalm, a moment of peace came over me, enabling me to complete my work. Thank God I was able to get through the day.

After work, I proceeded directly home. When I arrived, my mom and nana were patiently awaiting the arrival of the nurse who was scheduled to assist us in providing care for my granddaddy. They advised me to unwind, have dinner, take a shower, and get some well-deserved rest, as it would soon be my turn to assume the responsibility of caregiving. I did as they said. In order to give my granddaddy the care he needed, the four of us alternated in fulfilling the role of caregiver, ensuring that each of us had an opportunity to rest and recharge.

After my two-hour nap, my mom got some rest, leaving just me, Nana, and the nurse with Granddaddy. I sat by Granddaddy's bed and thought, "Wow, he looks so frail." I gently touched his forehead, kissed him, and held his hands while I prayed. I told him how grateful I was to have him as my granddaddy and remembered all the good times we'd had together, like when I made him bread pudding. Then, I felt a wave of gratitude wash over me, and I thanked God for the dream and for guiding me to stay home.

After spending a few hours with him, my mother returned and observed that I was becoming restless, so she took over my duties. I then went to take a nap. Approximately 30 minutes into my nap, my mother came to wake me up and, with tears in her eyes, she informed me that it was time. I looked at her with a puzzled expression and proceeded to get up and head to the room.

As I entered the room, the nurse and Nana were on the right side, while Mom and I were on the left. I distinctly recall my mother gently caressing my granddaddy's forehead as I held his hand. We all engaged in prayers and hymns as my granddaddy peacefully transitioned into the embrace of his Savior. It was at that moment that I comprehended the significance of my presence at home. God had guided me to be present during my granddaddy's father's final moments. As I stood there, overwhelmed with shock and with tears streaming down my face, a part of me departed with him.

"Count it all joy," although I must admit I did not experience joy in that particular moment. I was deeply hurt, saddened, and overwhelmed by a myriad of emotions. It left me feeling numb and disoriented.

Nevertheless, after taking the time to process and reflect, I came to the realization that God had granted me a little more time to spend with my granddaddy. To look after, to care for, and to converse with him. It was at that moment that I found joy in the present. I would have never thought that what I experienced with my granddaddy would prepare me for a future of encountering caregiving, grief, and loss.

Years later, when I was approximately 33 years of age, my grandmother came to live with us because her health was declining. She was suffering from dementia, and we had a rule in the house that whoever was awake would check on her to see if she needed anything. It happened to be me who got up to use the bathroom.

As I exited the bathroom and entered her room, I was immediately struck by a profound sense of God's presence urging me to stay close. I noticed that my grandmother had a striking resemblance to my late grandfather's frail appearance when he was confined to his bed.

Heeding this divine guidance, I started playing uplifting gospel music and engaged in heartfelt conversation with Nana. Once again, the Spirit guided me, prompting me to convey a message to my mom that something wasn't right.

She entered the room and noticed Nana. She immediately called for the nurse to come. In the meantime, my brother-in-law assisted me in making Nana comfortable. I had a strong feeling that I needed to be prepared for what was about to happen.

I was sitting by her bedside, holding her hand as we recited the 23rd Psalm together.

I leaned over and kissed her on the cheek as I shared my heartfelt gratitude for being my Nana. I told her how thankful I was for all the invaluable wisdom and pearls of knowledge she had imparted to me. Our cherished coffee and Bible discussions hold a special place in my heart. Nana played a pivotal role in introducing me to the Bible, and I was deeply grateful for the opportunity to spend this precious time with her. I discovered solace and contentment amidst the profound sadness of - Nana's final moments, finding comfort in her presence during that difficult time.

As the hymn "Old Rugged Cross" softly played in the background, my grandmother peacefully transitioned into the eternal embrace of her Savior. In that moment, I found solace in the present;

saddened by her passing, but relieved that she was no longer suffering.

Some time later, while in the process of streamlining my belongings, I discovered that I had retained the possessions of several deceased family members. By engaging in a systematic decluttering and downsizing endeavor, I experienced an enhanced sense of fulfillment and contentment. Throughout this process, I felt a profound healing effect taking place within me, as if they were conveying a message of reassurance, granting me permission to let go and acknowledging their state of peace.

You know, it felt like a weight off my shoulders when I released all that stuff that wasn't helping me grow as a person. It was like I was letting go of all the things that were holding me back, but I still held a special place in my heart for them.

As a life coach, I support my clients through questions, awareness, reflections, affirmations, and encouragement to co-create on a journey with them. I've also had to coach myself through some challenges. There was a moment when I paused to ask myself the same question I would ask my clients: "How would you eat an elephant?" The answer is one bite at a time. It was at that moment that I experienced a profound realization: I, too, am human, and I am deserving of the same compassion and understanding that I extend to others. It is acceptable to experience emotions, for we are all human.

We have to find joy in the midst of our adversities. Declaring the Word of God boldly with unwavering faith, believing that everything we desire shall come to pass. When your faith is tested under duress, know that God is using the circumstances to develop and strengthen your character.

The Passion Translation said it best:

James 1:2-4

"My fellow believers, when it seems as though you are facing nothing but difficulties, see it as an invaluable opportunity to experience the greatest joy that you can! For you know that when your faith is tested it stirs up in you the power of endurance. And then as your endurance grows even stronger, it will release perfection into every part of your being until there is nothing missing and nothing lacking."

Life is a gift, and there are lessons in our experiences that we glean and learn from. Every trial you endure will help you comfort others who are suffering from similar troubles.

Despite the numerous challenges and hardships that I have encountered throughout my life, I choose to view them in a positive light as opportunities for growth and learning. It has taken me some time to reach this mindset, but through a journey of self-discovery, gratitude, and introspection, I have come to appreciate the valuable lessons embedded within each experience.

So I'd like to ask you some reflective questions.

- What came up for you as you were reading this chapter?
- What's in your space that's causing you to feel adversity at this moment?
- What shift needs to happen to release the adversity?
- What must be done to move forward so that you always choose joy in the midst of adversities?
- What's my relationship to grief and loss?

(Journal it)

I would also like to offer some words of encouragement. Dealing with grief and loss, or any form of adversity, is an arduous journey.

I encourage you to seek divine guidance and direction through prayer. Humbly ask God to illuminate your path and guide you toward your next steps.

Take a moment to step back and identify the underlying cause of the situation. Reflect on what currently occupies your space and consider what actions you can take to address it.

Subsequently, develop a well-structured plan of action.

With unwavering determination and focus, diligently execute the plan.

When necessary, take a brief pause to thoughtfully reassess your progress and regroup.

Take deep breaths to maintain composure and a clear mind.

By all means, seek support from a trusted friend, minister, mentor, or professional, such as a therapist, counselor, or life coach, if you need it.

Additionally, you may consider joining a grief and loss support group. Remember, support is readily available to you. All you need to do is acknowledge your need for support, share your feelings, accept the help offered, take a moment to breathe, and be kind to yourself. Trust in the process and have faith that everything will turn out well. One resource you may want to check out is the website, griefshare.org. Here you can find in-person and online resources that can help you heal.

I hope these words provide some solace and guidance during this challenging time. Regardless of the challenges you encounter in life, I encourage you to meditate on the perspective outlined in James 1:2-4.

James 1:2-4 NKJV (New King James Version)

"My brethren, count it all joy when you fall into various trials, knowing that the testing of your faith produces patience. But let patience have its perfect work, that you may be perfect and complete, lacking nothing."

Thank you for reading this chapter. I pray an encouraging word was said that resonated with you to "count it all joy" in spite of your trials and tribulations.

May this closing Scripture bless you.

Numbers 6:24-26 New Living Translation

'May the Lord bless you and protect you. May the Lord smile on you and be gracious to you. May the Lord show you his favor and give you his peace.'

Amen.

The JOY of Friendship

By George D. Clanton

The JOY of Friendship

By George D. Clanton

It was a crisp, early fall morning and I was out walking my dog. It was really early, the sun had not quite come out, and the world was quiet. The air was clear. It was my favorite time of day. I use these early morning moments as a time to commune with nature and to speak with my Creator. We talk about all sorts of things. We talk about current events. We talk about how I am feeling about things. We talk about other people. I shake my head to Him and wonder why they do the things they do and I ask Him what lessons there are for me in what I am going through. I pray for and about my friends and family. But, no matter what is going on in my life or in the world, my thoughts and prayers always turn at some point to my father. I talk to him and I wonder what he would think about things that are happening here right now. Daddy passed through death into eternal life over 20 years ago. It was a Friday afternoon in October. It is hard to believe he has been gone so long. I am proud that his positive impact on my life is still prospering and impacting me every day.

So, most recently I was thinking about Daddy and wondering what he would think of today's gas prices. In his retirement years, he used to travel long distances to buy gas at low prices, which I used to tease him about. Was the juice worth the squeeze? He would burn up so much gas getting to the cheap gas! I have so many fond memories of him; but he was always clear that he was NOT my friend. He was my father. He would often express his love for me and he'd tell me that he was proud of me. Despite myself, this meant a lot to me. But these expressions were invariably accompanied by a caveat. We would chuckle together about this, too. He would always follow it up with, "I have to get on you sometimes…"

"You're a good boy. I'm proud of you. I have to get on you sometimes…"

"You're a good father. I like how you support what your children are up to. I have to get on you sometimes…"

I would ask why he always had to add that last part. He was never chagrined.

But, as I walked along the path that particular morning, I thought about grown man stuff and I wondered what Daddy, as a grown man, thought about things. Even though I was almost 40 years old when he went home to be with the Lord, I never really got to know him man to man. He was always Daddy and I was always his son. I wished there were friends of his I could talk with to get that perspective of who he was. As a grown man now, I have so many thoughts, feelings, doubts, insecurities, convictions. I often wonder how my father handled his. Perhaps, I won't know until we meet again. But, in the meantime, my thoughts turned to what God was trying to reveal to me in that moment. And then it hit me.

My best friend in this world passed through death to eternal life two years ago. He has a son and while it may be too late for me to hear stories from men my father was friends with, it is not too late for me to share my stories with my friend's son. So, this is a love letter in every sense of the word. Love inspired by my dad. Love motivated by my friend. Love for my friend's son. Love empowered by God.

This is important for me to share. It brings me a bittersweet joy to share the special moments that define a man – those moments that happen when no one is looking. Let me get started.

His name was Errick and we met on the campus of Howard University (HU). I noticed him long before he noticed me. He had on a sleeveless shirt that exposed muscular arms – not all cut like a bodybuilder, but unmistakably powerful. I watched him deal with the unfortunate gauntlet of confusion HU puts us all through as we try to register for classes. I had attended another university before transferring to Howard; so, I knew that what they were putting us through was crazy and that there was a better way.

It was a hot Monday in August of 1984. The day before, I had just gone with some buddies from high school to see this hot new movie called "Purple Rain." So, when the day started, I was in a good mood. By the end of the day, however, I had walked up and down that Hill so many times – I was really frustrated. The chaos starts at the Hilltop – the A building (A is for Administration). This building is named for Mordecai Wyatt Johnson, a noted scholar and athlete who was the university's first African-American president and successfully served in that role from 1926 to 1960! He held degrees from Morehouse, University of Chicago, and Harvard. With all that education, I wonder why he couldn't have established a more organized registration process for the students. My parents both attended Howard in the 1950's and they say it was the same way when they were there. But, I digress.

Throughout that day, Errick and I kept running into one another. We were both enrolled in Howard's School of Business, so we were taking a lot of the same classes. The process generally works like this: At the top of the Hill, we got our class schedule which would list the classes we were fully enrolled in. I had a professor named Collins for Accounting and one named Burnham for Computer Science. Oddly, the remaining 3 classes were all taught by the same Professor Tba. With a name like that, I figured he/she must have come from another country. Diversity, I thought, how cool! But no, and this is the first thing Howard taught me. "Tba" was not a name, it was an acronym that stood for "to be announced".

Getting into the Tba courses meant I had to go down the Hill to where the teachers' offices were, wait in long lines, and beg the teachers who taught the courses I needed to add me to their class rosters. If they agreed, then I had to go back up the Hill to notify the folks at the A Building, and then go back down the Hill again until I was properly admitted to each class on my schedule. For reasons I don't quite remember all these years later, my experience that day lasted all day long -- from 9:00am until 6:00pm. The last step was to get your picture for your student ID card. My picture looks like a mug shot. I was sweaty, exhausted and just wanted to go home.

I soon found out Errick was attending HU on a football scholarship because I overheard him explaining to one of the administrators that he was there asking for whatever he was asking for because this is what his coach had directed him to do. In the sea of frustrated faces and contention, he was calm and affable. He even managed to smile. He just knew what he needed and he kind of gleefully expected this person to help him out which, eventually, is how it all worked out.

Later, I was going into a building he was coming out of and we smiled at each other because we realized we had been running into each other all day. I don't remember introducing myself to him or him to me; but I feel like that shared smile was the beginning of a decades-long friendship that brought me so much joy.

After a semester or two together, Errick disappeared. There were problems at home in North Carolina that he had to take care of. Sometime later, he returned. I remember he called me on the phone. It was a nice reunion. I had not heard from him at all while he was away. Thankfully, we just picked up where we left off. By this time, he and his family agreed that football was distracting him from his studies and that he would be letting the athletic scholarship go. This meant his tuition would need to be paid without the assistance provided by that scholarship; so, money was going to be tight. Watching him during this season taught me important life lessons; lessons he would continue teaching me for the rest of his life. I learned that textbooks were books and there are books in the library. So, when the purchase of textbooks is not in the budget, they can be borrowed from the library. This is what he did, and he made it work.

Errick majored in Insurance and his first job out of college was at an insurance company. I don't remember much, but I do remember they were not kind to him there. One complaint was about the way he spoke. He was a country boy and, while he did not have a country drawl, he did sometimes have a way of saying things that were foreign to them. To this day, it still saddens me to think about his experience there, but I mention it only to highlight his resilience. He left that first company and found much success and acclaim at other companies where he was recognized and celebrated for his contributions. His resilience was a major theme in his life. When his son (or anyone) reads this, I hope it will stir the strength and resilience that lies deep within each of us so that we can persevere and find joy, no matter what life throws at us.

I truly admired Errick for his amazing resilience. He eventually left the insurance field, went back to school to study Information Technology (IT) and later found success here. He tirelessly shared his knowledge and skills to help his friends and his church with their IT needs. When the economy went bad and the job market was sketchy, he did what he had to do. At one point, he took a job that was about 75 miles from his home – making that daily commute, doing what he needed to do to put food on his table.

At another point, he took a job at Radio Shack – doing what he needed to do to make ends meet. Along the way, he shared touching stories with me of the compassion he shared with people. There was a young girl at Radio Shack who he encouraged as he told her about God's love for her.

On another job, there was a transgender man who, knowing that Errick was a Christian, was comforted to hear that he would be welcomed at any of Errick's church services. The stories go on and on.

Knowing him and having him as my friend brought joy into my life. He was smart and insightful. He spoke up when he needed to, and he also knew how to listen. He was confident in who he was. His son knows all the things he did and all the things he stood for. He remembers how he gave football pointers to his high school team. He remembers how he taught Sunday School. He remembers how he opened his home to friends and family. He remembers the deep love for his wife and for him. He remembers all of that. But he may not have been privy to the high regard, respect, admiration, and love that this man had for that man. He doesn't know all the episodes of life that built our strong bond.

Errick and both married the loves of our lives in 1990. I got married in June. He got married four months later in October. Very shortly after I got married, he helped me move from my apartment into hers. I remember him helping me carry a sofa up the stairs. He had one end, I had the other. He was walking forward. I was walking backward. Him being who he was, he suggested I turn around, carry the sofa with my hands behind my back so I could see where I was going. Me being who I was, I ignored him. Two steps later, I fell down. I had tripped over a step that I couldn't see. He was amused but there was no "I told you so" or anything like that. He just kind of smiled and I went on and carried it the way he had suggested in the first place.

Later in his life, Errick's health began to fail. His decline took a long, long time. He struggled with the ravages of diabetes, yet he never lost his praise. Despite all he went through, he never lost his joy; so, why should I lose mine just because he's not with us anymore? He would not want that.

One last story before I let you go. He and I used to participate in an annual concert called "When Black Men Sing to the Lord." It took place at this huge church and the tradition was for the men to stand shoulder to shoulder around the perimeter of the sanctuary as the closing prayer of Benediction was said at end of the program. Errick stood next to me. The prayer was said; but, when we opened our eyes, we realized that we were the only ones in this circle of over 100 men who were holding hands!

Anybody who knew Errick would say the following scripture was written with him in mind.

> *Romans 12:9-13 -- Love must be sincere. Hate what is evil; cling to what is good. Be devoted to one another in love. Honor one another above yourselves. Never be lacking in zeal, but keep your spiritual fervor, serving the Lord. Be joyful in hope, patient in affliction, faithful in prayer. Share with the Lord's people who are in need. Practice hospitality.*

I guess I can sum this all up by saying that Errick was exactly who he presented himself to be. He loved the Lord. He loved his family. He loved his friends. He wasn't one way on Sunday and another way through the week. He had that joy that the world can't give or take away.

He sought the Lord every day in every way. And as those of us he left behind continue on our journeys, we would do well to do likewise.

There is JOY and Beauty in Life's Challenges

By Dr. Genevieve Cromer

There is JOY and Beauty in Life's Challenges

By Dr. Genevieve Cromer

T.A. wasn't the first, the third, or fourth; T.A. was my number two son. He was a vibrant, busy, and curious child; he was always challenging. I should have known he would be, considering I made it to the hospital just in time to deliver him. I had to pay the hospital for just three minutes in labor and delivery. How did that happen, you ask? Well, it was August 23, 1986, and I was walking around, talking to my neighbors, just enjoying the beautiful day. When I finally decided to get ready to go to the hospital, my labor suddenly became intense, and I knew it really was time to go. I had been in labor since about noon that day, and now it was well into the evening.

T.A. always pushed the limits and did things his older brother, N.A., never considered. There was never a dull moment when T.A. was around. He loved playing with his older brother, which allowed me to do what I had to do as a stay-at-home mom. When T.A. was a little over one year old, I was in the family way again. In March of 1988, the younger brother, A.A., was born. T.A. was a great babysitter when I was not looking. He was always ready to share and care for his infant brother, even when he was resting.

Then, one day, when T.A. was 2 and a half years old, he was not his usual bubbly self. He moped around and was not hungry. If he ate anything, he would throw it up. That was very unusual for T.A., as he had an excellent, healthy appetite. As the day went on, he started to complain about feeling sick. That evening, I noticed that his urine was deep red, and I thought he might have had a urinary tract infection. I decided to put the boys to bed and planned to go to the doctor in the morning.

We did not have a car so, unless we got a ride, most of our traveling was done by bus, train, or foot. The Health Center that we went to was close to home and we could walk there, but that day it was a challenge. This was mainly because T.A. couldn't walk, he wanted me to carry him. His toddler brother was in the stroller, and his older brother, N.A., tried his best to help me by pushing the stroller. I was pregnant at the time, so carrying T.A. was no easy feat. We finally made it to the doctor's office, and I had to sit T.A. down. When we saw his pediatrician, which did not take long, she immediately knew something was out of the norm.

The pediatrician knew the boys were always in tip-top health at their yearly physicals. She sent us to Boston Children's Hospital immediately. We were put in a taxicab. I knew the situation was severe. After a long day and many different tests, all of which came back negative, the doctor finally drew fluid from T.A.'s spine, and the diagnosis was *Streptococcus pneumonia meningitis*.

"Pneumococcal meningitis can occur when the Streptococcus pneumonia bacteria invade the bloodstream, cross the blood-brain barrier, and multiply within the fluid surrounding the spine and brain. Viruses cause most forms of meningitis. Pneumococcal meningitis, however, is a bacterial form of meningitis. It's a serious disease that can cause death even with proper treatment."[2]

---

[2] Holm, G. (2023). Meningitis. Healthline: Meningitis. Retrieved from www.healthline.com

As a result of our pediatrician quickly sending us to the hospital, T.A. was there when some of the more severe side effects of this serious bacteria appeared. T.A. remained in the hospital for two weeks. Needless to say, this was not a happy time for T.A. Every day, I would pack lunch, and his brothers and I would get on the train and spend the day with him. In the beginning, he would be in an extended wheelchair. After about a week, he was steady enough to be on his feet. T.A. had physical therapy every day. Even though he had lost the usage of his right side, he stayed alert and gave the nurses and doctors a run for their money. At the end of our visits, which was at about 4:00 pm each day, T.A. would not want us to go. Thank goodness for Pee-Wee Herman's Movie. That movie captivated him, so he would calm down and I and his brothers could leave to head home. I asked T.A. what it was about that movie, which he still enjoys, and he said it made him happy. When T.A. was released from the hospital, he felt he could go back to what was normal for him. As the days moved along, he improved by playing with his brothers. There was a physical therapist for a brief period, but because of his young age and his desire and willingness to keep up with his siblings, he was able to regain his muscle usage. Soon he was able to do all of the things he'd been able to do before that bacterium invaded his young body.

A few months after T.A.'s sickness, it was time for N.A., his older brother, to go to school. When his brother went into the building on the first day of school, T.A. had a complete meltdown. At that time, son number three, A.A., was in a stroller, and I had a little over a month before baby number four was to be born. As we watched N.A. vanish behind the school doors, the meltdown began. I could not pry T.A. away. His shouts for his brother were loud and he refused to let go of the pole in front of the school that he'd grabbed hold of. I immediately began bargaining! T.A. drove a hard bargain, and it took me a while to coax him away. T.A. didn't want candy, he didn't want to see a movie or play with his toys, and nothing seemed to persuade him to want to leave and head home. He just wanted his brother. When he finally relented and we could go home, I felt like I had worked a full-time job. When we arrived home, he actually did want some of the things I had offered. Really? When it was time to get his older brother, T.A. ran toward him with the biggest smile. He hugged his brother as if he'd been gone for a long time. As the days passed, T.A. got better about allowing his big brother to attend school. At that same time, he was given the honor of being the caretaker of his younger sibling and that made him very happy. Another reason for his calmer demeanor might have been because he knew his brother would eventually come home.

My fourth son and bundle of joy was born in October. Now, I had all the Ninja Turtles: N.A., T.A., A.A., and it all followed up with G.A. Believe it or not, I learned that G.A.'s name means joy. Thank goodness for that; I was done!

Soon it was time for T.A. to go to school. What a difference between T.A. and N.A.; though his teachers loved him, he was challenging.

By this time we had moved and bought a house in another city. Three of the brothers were in school together. Shortly after the move, the boys' father and I legally separated and, eventually, we divorced. I decided to take the boys to therapy because I did not want them to think that the divorce was their fault. Closing in on about six months of treatment, T.A. revealed to the therapist that he had tried to kill himself and that the devil talked to him. I knew that he'd jumped out of the second-story window at our house, but I just nailed the windows shut so they could not open. Once he wanted to set himself on fire but, again, being what I thought was proactive, I hid all the matches. The therapist knew that we had to have T.A. evaluated once he told us what he had been thinking. Upon having T.A. evaluated, the mental health team decided that he was clinically depressed.

"Depression is a mood disorder that causes a persistent feeling of sadness and loss of interest. Also called major depressive disorder or clinical depression, it affects how you feel, think, and behave and can lead to a variety of emotional and physical problems. You may have trouble doing normal day-to-day activities and sometimes feel like life isn't worth living."[3]

On the day of the evaluation, I was told by his therapist beforehand to bring a suitcase so he could stay at the facility if the assessment came back with results that supported him remaining for immediate care.

It was a beautiful facility with horses, acres of land, and various patient activities. After meeting with the team that evaluated T.A., it was time to discuss the results and complete the paperwork I had to sign to leave my precious little boy there. When it was time for me to leave, T. A. looked at me and said, "Mom, you can go. I'll be okay." How could he say that to me? I was the mommy trying hard to provide what I thought was essential for him to thrive. My brain was racing! My heart was breaking! Oh Lord, help me! This part of being a mother was challenging! I did not want to leave my son, but I wanted my son to have a chance to grow up. Once I closed the door, knowing my child was not going home with me, my knees buckled, and I almost fell to the floor. One of my neighborhood friends, a wonderful woman who gave us a ride to the facility because my car was not running, was there to catch me. Why didn't I see what was going on with my child? I thought I was doing everything: loving, feeding, schooling him, attending church, going to therapy, everything. Why was this happening to my child, a boy who had already suffered from other challenges? I got myself together as my

---

[3] Mayo Clinic Staff (2024). *The Power of Body Language to Combat Depression*. Science of People. Retrieved from https://www.scienceofpeople.com/power-body-language-combat-depression/

neighbor drove home, and I wept through the quietness of the scenery we passed. My neighbor allowed me that quiet time as she drove us back home. I knew I had to get myself together because I had to tell his brothers what had happened and let them know that T.A. had to live apart from us for a while.

The facility had visiting days, and, of course, my car wasn't running. Luckily, the same neighborhood friend would allow me to borrow her car to go see my child. T.A. stayed in the facility for two weeks. I noticed the darkness under his eyes begin to lighten up. And once his journey was almost over, he asked to come home. I knew then that my child was ready and that he now had survival techniques that he could use as his life progressed. On his last night at the facility, T.A. invited us to dinner for Family Night, which he and the staff at the facility prepared for us. While he was there, the other boys continued with their group therapy sessions, and T.A. rejoined them when he came back home. They continued to see the therapist until she felt the boys were ready to be released. Well, who would have guessed that the boys tried to convince the therapist to allow them to continue for longer? Never mind, I was relieved I could check these sessions off my long list of things to do.

As T.A.'s educational journey moved forward, I noticed something different with him, something that I had not experienced with his older brother. The school they attended had weekly spelling tests, and while T.A. and I followed the same protocol I followed with his big brother when preparing together at home, T.A. didn't do well at all. His teachers noticed that T.A. seemed to mentally wander off and never wanted to answer questions, and when asked if he was okay, he would always say that he was. Finally, one of his teachers asked me to attend a parent/teacher conference. During the meeting, we discussed having T.A. assessed for disabilities. So, I had T.A. thoroughly evaluated. At that point, he was in the second grade, and we found that he was having difficulty with reading comprehension and with words. The diagnosis was that T.A. had dyslexia. Now that I was armed with information, I was ready to move ahead and aid T.A. with what he needed to succeed. What a relief to know that there could be a positive solution.

"Dyslexia is a learning disorder that involves difficulty reading due to problems identifying speech sounds and learning how they relate to letters and words, which is decoding. Also called a reading disability, dyslexia results from individual differences in areas of the brain that process language."[4]

"Dyslexia is not due to problems with intelligence, hearing, or vision. Most children with dyslexia can succeed in school with tutoring or a specialized education program. Emotional support also plays a key role. There is no cure for dyslexia; early assessment and intervention result in the best outcome. "[5]

The school the boys attended did not have the support that T.A. needed, so I found a school that did. He was placed in a specialized program for students with dyslexia. At the time, I was a teacher at the school the boys attended, and my focus was to get T.A. what he needed expeditiously. That meant my Ninja Turtles would be separated and not in the same school for a while. T.A. stayed in the program for students with dyslexia from the second grade to the fifth grade. Dyslexia does not dissipate. The beauty is that a person with dyslexia develops ways to conquer or overcome challenges as they grow and manage their educational journey.

---

[4] Mayo Clinic staff, dyslexia August 6, 2022. Retrieved https://www.mayoclinic.org/diseases-conditions/dyslexia/doctors-departments/ddc-20353559

[5] Mayo Clinic Staff, dyslexia August 6, 2022. Retrieved from https://www.mayoclinic.org/diseases-conditions/dyslexia/doctors-departments/ddc-20353559

During our early conversations, it was clear that T.A. was having difficulties in class. I asked him about it. He told me letters swam around on the board, things were confusing, and he did not understand what he read. Some of his work would need to be corrected because he would write some letters backward. I just listened and tried to be as understanding as possible. During the summer, I took an Orton Gilliam workshop so I would know better how to aid T.A. with his schoolwork. We got books on tape, and he studied that way. T.A. returned to school with his siblings, graduated from the eighth grade, and went on to high school. While in high school, we moved, and when T.A. felt he could not keep up with his peers, he lost interest in school. I finally realized that was not the way to go. I pulled him out and put him in a nontraditional school where he could work toward earning his GED.

After several disappointments with not passing the GED, I knew exactly what to do. I bought the GED study manual. When I first looked at it I just shook my head and said, "Oh my goodness, I have to devise a way to assist my son in getting through all of this!" So T.A. had a notebook, and he and I sat together for countless hours, not smiling at each other, but doing what had to be done. I went page by page, subject by subject, reading each content area in the manual unit. Eventually, we completed the manual. Whew! If you have never seen the GED manual, it has many pages and it's not easy to get through, but we did it and that made us both incredibly happy. The next time T.A. took the GED exam, he did so with a different, more positive attitude. A few weeks passed, and eventually T.A.'s scores were mailed. He passed!

Now, T.A. could attend school in Phoenix, Arizona. When I spoke to the program director, he told me it was hands-on instruction. It was all about welding, working with machinery, and building machines and motorcycles, and T.A. loved that hands-on way of learning.

Off to Phoenix, Arizona T.A. went, all alone. He was so excited to go and engage in a program that he had picked for himself. He had support, as his Godmother lived in Phoenix and wasn't too far from the school. However, his personality and tenacity did not allow him to call on his Godmother at all while he was there in school. He had his apartment, he had his food allowance, and he was able to move forward. It took him two years to complete the program. When he left school he moved to Boston, Massachusetts, while I was in Maryland.

Today, T.A. is a beautiful 38-year-old man. He recently decided to return to school and is now enrolled to learn coding. I applaud his "always-wanting-to-learn" attitude. He has a buddy attending school with him, and I know they will support each other. He is happy with this new chapter in his life. He always has had a fascination with machines. He is a designer, a tattoo artist, a welder, and an animal lover. He's strong, speaks articulately, and is extremely helpful. He intensely loves his family and is making it in the world. His laugh is infectious, and he is quite a charmer.

The joyful lesson of this story is that we have to stay positive throughout life's journey, even as the trials and tribulations occur. With a positive mindset, belief, and faith, my child grew up, entered the world, and now functions as a healthy adult. My four sons are now all grown up but they're still my Ninja Turtles and I'm extremely proud of each of them.

So, to the struggling families reading this, just remember: "Weeping may last through the night, but joy comes with the morning." Psalm 30:5

Keep your head up. My son didn't ask for his particular challenges, this is just what he had to live with, and he made it through. So can you.

The JOY That Comes With My Full Voice

By Valeria Elliott

The JOY That Comes With My Full Voice

By Valeria Elliott

At the age of 6, I made a 6-year-old decision to stop talking. This decision came out of my fear of getting into trouble, so I told myself to stop talking. That 6-year-old decision went on for 18 long and hard years.

At the age of 23, I became a Christian and asked God to give me my voice back and He did. Once I started talking again, I thought things would be much better, but they were not. I started hurting and mistreating people out of the hurt and pain I had endured over those 18 years of not talking. I had two people inside me -- the nontalker and the curser-outer. I did not want to go back to not talking again and I did not want to be the curser-outer. So, after going back on my knees a second time, I asked God to heal me from my past hurt and pain. God was so gracious. Not only did God heal me, but he also helped me find a happy medium between the nontalker and the curser-outer.

Over time things got better. I enjoyed having my voice back and speaking up for myself. OMG, not allowing anyone to talk over me and knowing that what I had to say was important felt amazing. I thought I was finally where I wanted and needed to be. But I recently realized I really hadn't regained my full voice. I was not always speaking up for myself and I was allowing certain family members to talk over me. That little girl who told herself to stop talking was still inside of me and she was choosing not to speak up for herself. Meanwhile, the curser-outer was sitting on my shoulders waiting to unleash and curse someone out. I didn't want her to come out again either.

One day I noticed I was having some of the same feelings I had when I first lost my voice. The feelings of not being heard, being talked over, feeling small and irrelevant. Those negative feelings made me realize I was missing a part of my voice. It took three different conversations with three family members to help me regain the fullness of my voice. With prayer and God's help, I knew I could get it back.

The first conversation wasn't as hard as I thought it would be. I needed to get some things off my chest and not worry about how the other person would react. The conversation started the same way, with this person talking and not allowing me to say anything. I prayed and asked God for the strength and boldness to say what I needed to say. In the past, after talking with her I would rerun the conversation over and over in my head wishing I had spoken up for myself. But not that day. This time the conversation was different. On that day I said what I needed to say without raising my voice or being hurtful. I felt so empowered and free. I found the courage to speak up for myself out of love for this person and for myself. Slowly I could feel that little girl regaining her full voice.

The second conversation was very different than the first. This family member has always been someone who was and is hard to get along with. In the past, I dealt with him out of fear, but not this time. Again, I prayed and asked God for the help I would need to have this difficult interaction. At the beginning of the conversation, I just listened, but when he started yelling at me I had to stop the curser-outer from coming out because I knew she was ready to share some choice words with him. Instead, I took a deep breath, quieted the curser-outer, and stopped him from yelling and cursing at me. I said what I needed to say with all the power and authority God had given me. He wanted to go back and forth with me, but I said no. I told him until he learned how to talk and treat me the way I deserved, we would no longer be having any conversation and I hung up the phone. I had to end the conversation because he wasn't used to me standing up to him, but I think he got the point this time. And again, I felt empowered and free, and my voice was getting fuller.

The last conversation was the most difficult of the three. This time, my emotional and mental health was at stake. This person had a habit of hurting my feelings and not caring that I was hurt. It got to the point where I realized that if I didn't speak up for myself and tell her how I felt, I would begin to hate her, and that wasn't what I wanted. I needed her to understand how she was persistently hurting me, and that I was no longer going to take it.

The conversation started as usual. We chit-chatted and laughed, and just when things were going well, she found a way to put me down. As I did in the previous two conversations, I prayed for God's help. However, this prayer was different. I asked God to allow me to speak to this person out of love, not anger or hurt. So I explained to her that no matter when we talked, she would always find a way to hurt my feelings and from that day forward that behavior would no longer be tolerated. Once the conversation was over, I asked God to heal me from the past hurt and I put those situations in the past where they no longer had the power to hurt me.

I have forgiven each one of those family members and have moved on. When I look back on these conversations I realize if these people hadn't continued to mistreat me, I wouldn't have realized I was missing my full voice and needed to get it back. Well, friends, I have my full voice, and I am using it to the glory of God!!!!!

I Find JOY In a Hobby

By Maurice K. Foushee

I Find JOY In a Hobby

By Maurice K. Foushee

During the years I spent dreaming about retirement, a period which lasted at least a decade, I remember hearing people say, "I don't know what I would do with myself if I retired." Or they'd ask, "What would I or could I do in retirement?"

While some retirees are fine without engaging in any organized or scheduled activity, others are constantly moving, whether physically or virtually, from one pursuit to another pursuit. Even a few people who are currently employed, and not anxious about or rushing towards retirement, often get bored or lost when considering anything beyond their jobs. Thankfully, I never worried about having something to do during my retirement years. That's because prior to leaving my full-time employment I found joy in a hobby that continues to interest me now that I've landed firmly and happily into retirement.

This magnificent hobby of mine is called numismatics. How is this pronounced? It is pronounced as *noo-miz-MAT-iks*. What is numismatics? You mean you have not heard about it? I'm sure you've heard of it, but you might know it by its more common name – coin collecting. Numismatics includes the study and collection of coins, paper money, medals, and tokens. Hearing about this hobby might elicit chuckles, yawns, or questions such as, "What is so fascinating about that?" or, "Why do you find joy engaging in it?"

I find mental and emotional refuge and relaxation through coin collecting. I find refuge from reading about it in solitude or while waiting for an appointment. I focus on the periodicals to which I subscribe rather than some television programs or annoying commercials. Relaxation occurs when I read because that means I am not in a meeting, writing a report, or preparing for a presentation. Upon seeing nice, and sometimes amazing, designs of currencies, I can observe art and become an art critic, of sorts, without obtaining certification.

Numismatists typically like art, history, geography, politics, zoology, or a combination of these subjects. Based on their designs, coins, paper money, medals, and tokens often tell stories about individuals, regions, and societies. It has been referred to as "the hobby of kings" because, until about the last century, it was usually royalty and nobility who collected coins. This was, in part, because they were the few who could afford to assemble a collection. Currencies represent the culture, features, and aims of issuing nations. Changes in designs and denominations sometimes track changes in social, political, and economic conditions.

One of the joys of numismatics is that it appeals to various personality types, both extroverts and introverts enjoy it. Extroverts speak at events, share their finds or knowledge in-person or through social media, or actively join coin clubs. Introverts enjoy their collections privately at home by quietly reading publications or discreetly following social media posts. The hobby also draws interest across generations. Many collectors' curiosity, including mine, began when they were children. Some pursue this pastime throughout their lives, while others focus on other interests or on life obligations and then return to the hobby. Depending on interests, time for research, and personal ambitions, the hobby can offer investment prospects. Furthermore, its fascination spans across nationalities, race, gender, and income.

Numismatics is an international pursuit as nations produce unique currencies that attract at least a few collectors worldwide. It offers me an opportunity to "travel" domestically and internationally without having to leave my home as I view and admire coins and currencies from varying locations, subjects, and with different histories. Have you visited South Africa, Namibia, Ethiopia, South Sudan, Nepal, Laos, Oman, India, or China? Through banknotes and coins, I have briefly toured these and several other nations. I can admire their wildlife, landscapes, landmarks, and historical figures simply by looking at their money.

I have enjoyed the remarkable world of numismatics. It has provided me with many opportunities to learn about this nation and the world, and to appreciate aesthetics in metal and paper forms. Hopefully, you have found or will soon discover a hobby that will mentally, emotionally, or physically captivate you, too.

JOY Comes Through Acceptance

By Heather M. Hammond

JOY Comes Through Acceptance

By Heather M. Hammond

"I am sorry to inform you that your biopsy result is complete, and it is positive for cancer." These were the words spoken to me over the phone by the radiologist who had performed my biopsy a few days before. The biopsy was performed because my mammogram done three weeks earlier resulted in suspicious findings in my left breast. At that point I was told that I should get a biopsy. I wasn't worried. I felt everything would be okay and the biopsy result would come back just fine. I expected that I would continue to move along in my life as usual. Wow, was I wrong.

Right after the radiologist informed me that I had cancer, the first words out of my mouth in response to her news were, "Oh no, I can't believe that. It can't be. Are you sure?" I naively thought that maybe the hospital's lab had made a mistake or maybe the radiologist called the wrong patient and gave me someone else's results. I was surprised by the call because I'd had only one mammogram in my entire life. How could my first and only mammogram result in a cancer diagnosis? Secondly, I felt fine. Other than my seasonal allergies and mild asthma I didn't suffer from any major medical illnesses. I didn't view myself as a sickly person. I was no "spring chicken" but, in my early forties, I was not elderly either. I was active and energetic. Lastly, another reason it was hard for me to believe my results was simply because I could not wrap my mind around the idea of me being a cancer patient. That was in no way part of the plans I had for my life. I am a registered nurse. I felt like it's always been my job to take care of patients. I was not accustomed to being a patient. I felt like I was not ready for that new role.

I couldn't sleep the night I received that phone call. I sat up all night with different thoughts racing through my mind. I asked myself how I was going to be able to deal with cancer. I worried about how my diagnosis would affect not only me, but also my young daughter, Marie. As a single parent, I realized that a lot of the plans I had for us would have to be modified, changed, or canceled. I didn't want my diagnosis to be a burden for her. My major concern was for her.

After the first few days of hearing my medical diagnosis, I was soon able to process things more clearly. I realized the most important thing I had to do was to put God first in my battle against cancer. I understood there was no way I was going to make it through any surgery, treatment, medication regimens or therapies without submitting to the will of God and praying to and calling on God throughout my cancer journey.

After putting God first, I then realized I had to come to a point of acceptance. I needed to mentally, emotionally and spiritually accept that I had a deadly disease and that I was going to have a difficult health battle to fight through. I had to accept that I was going to have to alter a lot of my plans and modify a lot of my routines. The Bible says in 2 Corinthians 5:17, "Therefore, if anyone is in Christ the old has passed away, the new will come." Most of us do not like change, especially if a change is forced upon us. A lot of times, we want to keep doing the same things, the same ways. We want to keep going to the same places, have the same friends, and keep the same jobs for as long as we can. We want to keep doing the things we like and that make us comfortable. But sometimes we can't. The only thing that does not change is God and His word. Hebrews 13:8 says Jesus Christ is the same yesterday today and forever.

In life, if we are blessed to live long enough, we have to embrace the fact that changes are inevitable. I had to accept that changes were going to have to be made in my life and in the life of my daughter in order for me to best handle my diagnosis. And things were changing fast.

Friends, I am here to tell you that no matter the circumstances, acceptance can help lead us down the pathway toward joy. When something difficult happens or an unexpected trying time occurs, like the death of a loved one or some other major disappointment in our lives, we often feel like we have lost control and our life is going awry. We might develop a feeling of "doom and gloom" and experience anger, fear and/or sadness. All those emotions can be valid. Even if we are people with a strong faith in the Lord, we should not feel guilty for experiencing such a range of emotions.

Acceptance allows you to take control of your emotions and focus on what is ahead of you and what is important to you. Acceptance helps us avoid giving into the negatives or giving up on hope. Acceptance means you understand who you are as a person, whose you are, what your needs are, and can identify the resources you have and those you may need to find. I realized I had to accept my own personal circumstances head on, both the positives and problems.

You can try to run from your problems. You can try to run from people. You can move from city to city. You can successfully do all those things, but you cannot successfully run from God. God our Father, Jesus Our Lord and Savior and The Holy Ghost Our Redeemer will only be given the ultimate rightful position in our lives when we accept them. God gives us free will, but He wants us to accept Him and His ways, even if we do not always understand them.

A few times, I have gotten caught up in my feelings and have had a false sense of entitlement. When I first started my painful medical treatments there were times when I felt I didn't deserve to be so sick. I felt severely depressed, and I didn't feel much joy. A false sense of entitlement keeps us from accepting the will of God in our lives. An inflated or wounded ego can keep us from embracing the concept of acceptance. It will make us feel we deserve more, we should have more, we should be more, and that's not always healthy. It makes us feel we shouldn't have to deal with anything difficult in life. That type of ego can leave us with bitterness, resentfulness and jealousy when dealing with hardships. When all three have a prominent part in our psyche, they separate us from experiencing joy in our lives. They separate us from God who is the ultimate joy of our lives. Jeremiah 29:11 says, "I know the plans I have for you; declares the Lord, plans to prosper you and not harm you, plans to give you hope and a future." God accepts us with love as his children, we need to accept God with love in return.

I had to start accepting my past (instead of running from it). That included facing the past highs and heartbreaks, my mistakes and achievements, and I had to better understand the true nature of the relationships in my life. If I had never started down my road of really accepting myself, fully embracing who I am and what my personal journey has been, I would have continually felt lost and down. I would have kept going around the circles of my disappointment and I would have never been able to accept where I was in life. Once I started the process of acceptance and I started trying to live life as it was presented to me, with both the good and the bad, I started feeling more joyful. It was when I stopped running from my problems and started facing my issues head on, all while surrendering to God's will, that I found joy -- and joy found me.

While in the midst of my cancer journey, I've become more accepting of myself and more in tune with my feelings. Walking in acceptance has allowed me to understand more about my insecurities (things I've felt since childhood), about my strengths, and led me to be more honest with myself about my decades-long (since I was teenager) off and on relationship I had with my ex-boyfriend/friend. It's allowed me to be more hopeful about making plans for my future, in spite of dealing with current difficulties. And I better understand that God still wants what is best for me. Before I started accepting the truth about those things, my true joy was being blocked and I didn't even realize it.

We all crave acceptance. We all want to be liked, we want to be wanted, and we sometimes need validation. It's nice to be accepted by our friends or family or people around us. It can give us temporary satisfaction. Temporary satisfaction can feel good. But it's just that, temporary. The issues come when we don't accept ourselves. And the biggest problem is when we don't accept God. I don't care how many friends a person has or how many material items they have, if they don't accept themselves or accept Jesus as their Lord and Savior, they will not have any real joy in life. In John 14:6 Jesus said "I am the way and the truth and the light. No one comes to the Father except through me."

I love the Lord. I am thankful for the path God continues to keep me on. I am on a continual journey of learning to have more self-acceptance, more self-love and to do more self-discovery. I am learning every day how to be more accepting of and more empathetic toward other people. I am learning more every day how to accept God, accept His ways, accept His will and accept His word. I'm learning every day more how to teach my daughter these things as she continues to grow.

I am a work in progress. I fall short of my goals sometimes and sometimes I mess up. Sometimes I sin, sometimes I say or do the wrong things. I am constantly growing, learning, evolving and maturing. One thing I do understand without a doubt is that through my acceptance of Christ comes my real joy. No cancer, no medical diagnosis, no other person, no circumstances can take that away from me. That joy gives me my ability to appreciate a long walk in a garden, maintain hope, enjoy playing with my daughter at the park, enjoy a sunrise breakfast on the beach, enjoy dancing at a party, appreciate going to a new restaurant or laughing with a friend. It also allows me to even be able to crack up at my own corny jokes sometimes. LOL! We must constantly choose joy!

My Village of JOY

By Irma D. Hinton

My Village of JOY

By Irma D. Hinton

When life is life-ing all around you and your world is spinning and spiraling, it is imperative to have people you know, love and respect close by. You need people you can turn to for support, encouragement, and prayer. I consider these people parts of "My Village."

You may recall the old saying, "It takes a village to raise a child." This is an African proverb that means it takes many people, "the village", to provide a safe, healthy environment for children to grow. They need help from the village to develop, flourish, and realize their hopes and dreams. I grew up with that kind of village watching over me, protecting me, providing much needed, and sometimes unwanted advice. They chastised me when I was wrong, whipped my behind when necessary, but they also celebrated and supported me when I succeeded. My village is made up of people whom I love, respect, and trust. Without them, I do not know where I would be today.

My village is not huge, but just large enough to give me what I need and do what I need it to do. My village has been there for me. They consist of everyday, regular people who have seen me through some tough times, fun times, challenging and sometimes unbearable times. I consider them my families and when I pull them together, they make up my village.

My village consists of my immediate and extended DNA biological family, people who know me and how I was raised. They protected me when others tried to hurt or take advantage of me. They trained me and looked after me, even when they did not want to. They got me in trouble while at the same time kept me out of trouble. With these people in my life, I had the best childhood any kid could ask for. I did everything a kid was supposed to, which included having fun and enjoying my childhood. I was raised to be respectful to my elders, teachers, preachers, and law enforcement. I had the freedom to run around the neighborhood, but always stayed within earshot of my mom. I visited my grandparents and relatives in Rocky Mount, North Carolina, once or twice a year. My siblings, cousins, and I had the best times when we were together, especially during our family reunions. My mom was a firm disciplinarian, and she sprinkled it with all the love a kid could ever want or need.

Then, there is my Northeast (NE), Washington, DC neighborhood family. They consist of friends and neighbors I grew up with through elementary, junior high and high school in NE neighborhoods around 2nd, 3rd, 4th, 5th and E, F, G and H Streets. I still see many of them regularly and we are still active in each other's lives 40 and 50 years later. Unfortunately, so many of them have passed on, but we keep the connection going and continue to support each other whenever and however we can. We participate in activities that bring us together, sometimes annually and sometimes more often. These are the people that I ran up and down the streets of DC with as a child, playing double-dutch, hide and seek and hopscotch, riding bikes, building go-carts, jumping across rooftops, playing flag football (kids against the adults), and putting on talent shows. We went to house parties, school dances and GoGos (music unique to DC's culture) in the park. Even now we are very active in our high school alma-mater's football and homecoming games and participate in all fundraising events.

Next, there is my Army family, another important part of my village. They consist of good, generous, kind people who I respect and adore. I served my country with them in the Regular and Reserve Army. I truly cherish the bonds we formed while serving our country, whether in the US or abroad. We did something extra special, something that not everyone can or is willing to do. We stood up and raised our hands to serve and protect our country in uniform against all enemies, foreign and domestic, with pride, honor, and dignity. We signed up to put our lives in harm's way for our country and fellow man. These are the bravest people I know, and I deeply respect them. I connect with some of them every month to fellowship and reminisce about old times and all the antics that kept us in tears laughing constantly. We also have our annual reunion in Maryland that includes all the former units in the Brigade. This is a grand time for us because we get to see so many others that we have not seen in a very long time, and honor those that are no longer with us. My time served in the military was one of the best and proudest times of my life and I hope I never forget it.

Then there is my church family. These people ground me in my Christian faith and feed my spiritual needs through the preaching and teaching of the word of God. Together we sing praises and worship unto the Lord, which automatically encourages and lifts my spirit. I can count on them to pray for me during trials and tribulation. When I am unsure or confused, I know that Jesus is the way, the truth, and the life (John 14:6). When I am feeling down or defeated, I know I can do all things through Christ that strengthens me (Philippians 4:13). I share a special bond with a few of my choir members and those that I have served with on church ministries and outreach activities. These people are part of my prayer circle, and they make themselves available when I've asked for or needed prayer.

The final family included in my village is my Sistah Circle. It is composed of women from all the previous families I mentioned. Every woman should have girlfriends they can call or go to for encouragement and support; to vent, to laugh, to cry or just to talk things over with to help you make sense of things and provide perspective and clarity. They are all special to me in one way or another, and they all bring something different into my life. We worship together, travel together, celebrate birthdays and anniversaries, recognize each other's accomplishments and successes, party together, and also provide a shoulder for each other to cry on if necessary.

These distinct groups of people, these families, have supported, consoled, encouraged, laughed, cried, and most of all prayed for me. They are near and dear to my heart, and I am truly blessed to have them in my life. We may not always get along or agree with one another, but the bond is never broken. It may become a little scratched, but we always seem to come back from those times and continue as if nothing ever happened. It is wonderful to know that people love you unconditionally and will be there for you if you allow them. I am thankful and grateful for all who make up my remarkable Village of Joy.

The World's Fair and the JOY of An Extended Family

By Magdalene Johnson

The World's Fair and the JOY of An Extended Family

By Magdalene Johnson

Before I started school, I was cared for by Sarah, a nice woman who lived around the corner from my family. My brother, Raynard, was responsible for getting me to and from Sarah's home. I gave him hell each and every day. I didn't want to go to Sarah's in the mornings and I did not want to leave her home in the evenings. Sometimes, after a particularly stressful time with me during the afternoon pick-up, my brother would leave and patiently return to pick me up later in the evening. That's how stubborn I could be.

Eventually I matured and didn't have the same morning or afternoon drama. I started elementary school during the 1963-1964 school year, and I walked to and from school with my brother, Isaiah, who was in the 5th grade. We attended Lakeland Elementary School, the local school located just a few blocks from our home. My first-grade teacher was Mrs. Gantt. Lakeland Elementary School had once been a high school and was one of the first schools in Prince George's County, Maryland that allowed Black students to attend.

The school is located in Lakeland, a Black community in College Park, Maryland. My mother was born and raised there along with her siblings -- a sister, brother, two half-brothers, and a half sister. They all called their father Mr. Russell, because that's what they heard their older half-siblings call him. Both of my mother's parents, Charlie and Azora, had been married previously and they combined their families when they got married. Mr. Russell worked on the streetcars for D.C. Transit, but he drank and was unreliable. So my mother left school when she was young and found work as a domestic so that she could help out with family responsibilities.

It was during World War II that my mother met my father, who had joined the service before the War broke out. My father was from Massies Mill, VA, where he grew up with four brothers. Several of his brothers had left Massies Mill and made it to Washington, DC and further east. This next part of this story may sound like a Hollywood movie, but it is the beginning of my family.

My mother and father met in the summer of 1943 (August to be exact) and got married in September of 1943. I guess they enjoyed their honeymoon because my oldest brother, Leo, was born May 30, 1944. There were several babies after that, Limatine (1948), Raynard (1951), Isaiah (1953) and I. Two babies were lost in infancy. My family lived with my grandparents until my father questioned what would happen to him and his children if something happened to my mother. Soon thereafter, my parents noticed a lot for sale in College Park, Maryland and decided to purchase it and build a house. The house was completed in 1955, around the time my brother Isaiah was two years old. I came along two years later.

The house was just big enough for us all. My parents and I had bedrooms on the lower level and my brothers slept in the largest bedroom upstairs. I really don't remember too much about the time that Leo was there because he joined the army in June 1962, right after graduating from high school. I do remember him working with electronics, which came in handy later in life. Leo and my brother Limatine once took an old speaker and turntable, along with some wiring, and created a radio station! They had an entire show where they announced the weather and played music. After a while they started getting requests from people in the neighborhood. This went on until my father read in the paper about how the FBI was going to charge a family in Virginia with FCC charges for doing the same thing that my brothers were doing. That's when the radio station was permanently shut down. However, both Leo and Limatine went on to create radios as science projects in school. Now, getting back to my first year in school…

I was anxiously anticipating the end of that school year because it had been decided months before that my two youngest brothers and I were going to spend the first part of the summer in New York City. Most people were going to "the country" in those days, but we were going to the Big Apple. How did that come about? Well, my father's younger brother, Albert (Pete) and his wife, Thelma, had moved to Brooklyn after the War. I loved the times when Uncle Pete and Aunt Thelma came to visit and stayed with us. During one of those visits, they'd invited us up for the World's Fair and now that trip was about to happen. Aunt Thelma was one of my favorite aunts, along with my Aunt Irene (my mother's sister and my godmother).

By the time Friday, June 12th came around we couldn't keep our enthusiasm from showing. We had been shopping for new clothes and other needs over the previous few weeks, we were ready to go. My mother was working, and my father was doing things with the Boy Scout troop where he served as Assistant Scout leader and was also helping out at church because it was going to be Children's Day that following Sunday. Also, my mother's cousin, Etta from Baltimore, was visiting her sister Bernice who lived in our neighborhood, too. It was a really busy weekend.

Everything had gone without a hitch that Sunday at the First Baptist Church of College Park and my family and I were back at home having dinner. Sometime after dinner my father got a phone call from Bernice's husband asking my father to ride with him to take Etta back to Baltimore that night. He had asked a neighbor to go with him, but that neighbor decided it was too late to go. My father agreed and they planned to leave at about 8:30pm. Of course I wanted to go, too, but it was so late that my father told me I couldn't go. I didn't understand the problem with me going, and the scene I made was not pretty. My brothers tried to calm me down and eventually we went inside to clean the kitchen before going to bed. I slept upstairs with them that night and do not remember waking up until about 8am the next morning. That's when we heard the knocking at the front door.

Standing at the door were my Aunts Pauline and Irene and my Uncle Will Lee. They'd come to tell us that our parents had been in a car accident while returning from Baltimore and that our father had died. They went on to tell us that our mother wasn't in great shape either. The car they were in was hit by a drunk driver who had beer cans and liquor bottles on the floor of his car. This man ran directly into the Ford my father was driving. My mother was sitting in the back seat directly behind him. Apparently, the impact broke my father's neck. Seat belts weren't the law at the time. On impact, my mother hit her head on something, and glass engulfed her. Her left ear was nearly sheared off. The other two passengers in the car my father was driving weren't seriously hurt and didn't need medical attention.

At a point right after the accident, my mother recalled saying something to my father, not knowing that he had died. She didn't find that out until she was in the hospital and asked how the man was doing. That's how she found out that my father had died.

My parents were both driven to St. Agnes Hospital in Baltimore, Maryland. I don't know if it would have made any difference, but they were much closer to Laurel Hospital, but that hospital didn't take "Colored People" at the time. It was just so much for me to take in and when I needed someone the most, it seemed as if no one was there.

We were all shattered, but I don't remember my brother Raynard crying at all, at least not in my presence. Years later I learned that our father had asked him to take care of me, so I just assumed that Raynard suspected something was going to happen.

My two closest friends, my neighbor Jackie and my cousin Vanessa, helped me make it through those days. Vanessa's mother, my Aunt Irene, had more or less moved into our house to help care for us. I cannot remember much about that long week leading up to the funeral, but my Uncle Pete and Aunt Thelma came down to help with arrangements and they visited with my mother in the hospital. I remember that they had to get the National Guard involved in locating my brother Leo because he was on a special assignment in the Gulf of Iran. I also remember when my Aunt Irene took Vanessa and me to my father's viewing at the church that Thursday. I remember seeing so many people. I even saw Mrs. Gantt, my first-grade teacher.

It was hard seeing my father that way. I kept thinking about the times we shared, just the two of us, like the times he took me to a nearby dairy to get ice cream cones. It was later decided that Vanessa nor I would be allowed to attend the funeral. We were left with relatives of Vanessa's father and later picked up to join our family at Arlington National Cemetery, where my father was buried. I remember that the repast was held outside and that one of our neighbors, who was a builder, had supplied multiple picnic tables. He left one of those tables for us to keep.

Many of our neighbors and family attended the services and the repast, but my mother wasn't able to attend. We were very worried about her. We had gotten progress reports from the hospital, but we just weren't going to be OK until we saw her. My mother's ear was saved by a cosmetic surgeon, who was studying at John Hopkins University and later became very famous. Unfortunately, I cannot remember his name. She could never have her ears pierced because of the chipping off of skin on her left ear. Eventually Uncle Pete and Aunt Thelma brought my mother home, and her entire head was wrapped in bandages. She had multiple scars over her body and was still removing glass from her hair and skin. We spent that summer making trips to the drug store to get cocoa butter to help heal her scars. We were basically our mother's nurses, and we got help from our neighbors. My brother Leo had tried to get discharged from the service, indicating he had to help care for his family. My mother insisted that he stay, saying that he had to finish what he started, so he completed his service.

As you'd imagine, my mother was worried about a variety of things, but she took her time deciding what to do. Social Security indicated she could stay home and get paid a monthly allotment for the youngest children and herself, but my mother wanted to continue to work. She got a job at a newly opened department store not far from where we lived, Woodward and Lothrop, and was pleased to know that benefits would be provided. She also got a lawyer to sue the man that caused the accident. (Yes, the drunk driver had survived, but barely.) The insurance company decided to go to trial because they indicated that my mother's cousin, Bernice, had mentioned that my father had taken a drink at her sister's house in Baltimore. In the end, it was determined that he had not, but it sure did cause a rift between my mother and her cousin for years. They finally made up when Bernice was sick with breast cancer. The lawyer for our family eventually won the case and there was a settlement amount, which my mother put in the bank. Also, there was a settlement for us kids, where funds were deposited for us each month until the last one of us turned 18 years old.

In the midst of everything going on, my mother decided to learn how to drive. She easily passed the written part of the test, but I think she failed the driving portion five times before passing because she had trouble parking. (Hahahaha!) I had to give her a break though, she was almost 40 years old.

As the next school year began, family and friends continued to check on us and everything was working well, even though we all missed my father dearly. But our extended family was there for us. They visited with us on a regular basis and were very involved in ensuring our well-being.

My mother eventually bought a car that satisfied the size of the family. She still didn't like to drive, but she did so to survive and take care of her family.

By January 1965, we found out that Leo and Abby, his high school girlfriend, were going to get married. My mother was not happy, but Abby was pregnant. Limatine tried his best to talk Leo out of it, but it didn't work. The wedding was on a snowy Sunday. It was held at Abby's parents' house, but Limatine nor I attended. Abby's father, who was a preacher, officiated. The newlyweds honeymooned in New York City and stayed with our Uncle Pete and Aunt Thelma. As the year went on, my nephew Chris was born on the 15th May of 1965.

It was about this time that we were hearing talk of a trip to New York City, but I did not have my hopes up. I didn't believe we were going until we were leaving the house to catch the Greyhound bus on New York Avenue in downtown Washington, D.C. My mother had packed her three youngest children, as well as our cousin Vanessa, and loaded us all up to go to NY to go to the World's Fair. This was just over a year after my father died. We were all so excited, even my mother was excited. Both Uncle Pete and Aunt Thelma were waiting at the station when we arrived. They loaded us all in their Chevy and took us home to their townhouse in Brooklyn, where we stayed for the next week. It was all that I had imagined, all the bright neon lights and their home in Brooklyn on just a regular neighborhood street. We went to the World's Fair on several different days, it was held in Flushing Meadows that year. I still remember the steel atlas of the world that I first saw there. (Now you can see it at the US Open stadium.) I have many fond memories of us going out to Coney Island during that visit, the rides and, of course, the food we enjoyed. My uncle drove us around the city and we visited family in Harlem. My aunt's Siamese cat, Dirtyface, had just delivered kittens, so of course I asked to have one. That's where my love of cats began. Dirtyface lived to be 23 years old.

That was a wonderful trip that I never expected after what had happened the year before. We returned home to a shell of a go-cart in the backyard that Limatine had purchased. My mother regretted later letting him keep it. After he got the motor, it was a total nightmare. Life was getting back to normal.

That trip to NY and the events leading up to it made me realize how important family is. Having a family that reaches out to you and makes you feel wanted is priceless and that's why I have always been so close to my father's side of the family. As years passed, I spent many Christmas holidays in Brooklyn. On several trips to New York, we traveled with Uncle Jack who was blind but gave the best directions. He'd ask us the name of the street we were on and then get us to our destination every time. I also made trips to my father's hometown, Massies Mill, on several occasions.

Later in the summer of 1965, shortly after that memorable trip to the World's Fair, I was outside playing in the yard with my friend Jackie, when a big delivery truck pulled up. It unloaded a carrier right in front of my house. To my delight, it was holding one of those kittens I'd met in Brooklyn, the exact one I had selected. I named her Snow White.

It was in the wake of tragedy that I got a glimpse of the joy that comes from extended family and an unexpected trip.

The JOY of a Family Legacy

By Maria Miller Johnson

The JOY of a Family Legacy

By Maria Miller Johnson

For as long as I can remember, both my maternal family, the Kimbroughs, and my paternal family, the Millers, have held family reunions. The Kimbroughs have gathered every year in Statesville, NC for the Willian Gaston and Clara Kimbrough Family Reunion. The Millers have gathered every other year in South Carolina for the Milton and Millie Miller Family Reunion.

The first Kimbrough Family Reunion was hosted by my grandmother, Connie Kimbrough Spicer, and her siblings. It was held at her home on Eastside Drive in Statesville, NC. But just how did this all come about?

The family patriarch, William Gaston Kimbrough, was born in Kimbrough, Ala. He was a proud Black man and was an entrepreneur. At an early age he traveled to Trenton, New Jersey, where he met the woman who would become his wife, Clara Van Schiver. They married and had three children while living in Trenton, New Jersey. Several years later, in the early 1900's, the family relocated to Statesville, North Carolina. Gaston built his family home in Statesville and later purchased land on what is now Greenbriar Road, in the Belmont community of Statesville. He used the land in Belmont for farming. William Gaston Kimbrough, affectionately known as Papa, believed in family and in supporting and providing for his family.

When his family increased in size, William bought more land in the Arbor Woods Community of Statesville, near Eastside Drive. He also purchased some farm animals. He opened the first General Store in the community near Old Salisbury Road and furnished the store with goods from his farm. He operated the store using his own money and generously offered credit to many of his loyal customers so they could get what they needed.

Ultimately William and Clara had 14 children. Most of their children were farmers, educators and entrepreneurs, and they each left a legacy for their children.Their eldest child was my grandmother, Connie. Connie married Robert Lee Spicer. Born to this union were two daughters, however one child did not survive. The surviving daughter, Alma, my mother, was raised an only child, however, Connie helped to raise several of her nieces throughout the years.

Connie was a master teacher, planner, organizer and motivator. She had a gift of managing and organizing things and she did it well. I guess it either came to her naturally or it came from the practice she likely got having had 13 brothers and sisters. It brings me joy to know that my grandmother was an accomplished educator, motivator and was also a respected community leader, especially within the school system in Statesville. She was also a leader in the Women's Federation Organization there. She taught critical thinking skills and encouraged people within her community to step outside of their comfort zones and accomplish great things. She had a positive impact on a lot of lives in that area.

One story I remember hearing over the years is about how her daughter, my mother, was one of her students at Unity School and how she did not give her any leniency just because she was her daughter. There was no favoritism with Connie.

Another story I remember is about how my grandmother gave my mother an assignment to make a Cinderella ball gown out of a parachute. Alma asked, "You want me to make what?" Connie replied, "You can make it!" Alma said, "Where's the pattern?" Connie then told her that she could make the pattern. So, Alma proceeded to study pictures of the gown and looked at various patterns and was eventually able to make her own pattern for the fairy tale ball gown, which was later used for a play.

Once Connie was asked to prepare a luncheon for the annual meeting of supervisors at Unity School. She included her students in the preparations and trained them in etiquette while doing so. The class planned the menu, prepared the three-course meal, set the tables with crystal and china, served the guests, and cleared the banquet room at the end of the event. It brings me much joy to know that my grandmother maintained a standard of excellence in everything she did. At the time her students probably did not understand the high standards she was setting, but I'm sure they later appreciated the training that they gained under her tutelage. It was important to her that they become independent thinkers who weren't afraid to try new things. I guess you could say that Connie's ability to do what she loved, educating students on home economics, meant that she never worked a day in her life. This love of educating earned her the Presidential Award and Teacher of the Year Award by 17 Magazine. Her daughter, Alma S. Miller, followed suit by never working a day in her life while educating students in the public school system in Washington, DC. She, too, earned the Presidential Award for Teachers.

I once had the opportunity to meet one of my grandmother's students in the most unlikely place. I was working at a dialysis center in Washington, DC and, while completing an initial assessment, I discovered that the patient was one of my grandmother's former students. What a surprise to meet someone who knew her in the educational setting and who held my grandmother in such high regard. It also reinforced within me the need to provide my dialysis clients with the utmost care and respect because you never know who you're talking to. Like my grandmother, I want to maintain a level of excellence, I could be talking with an angel unaware.

The Milton & Millie Miller Family originated in South Carolina. Milton and Millie had eight children, and I am a descendant of Wesly Miller. My great-grandfather, Wesley Miller, was a farmer in South Carolina and his wife was a homemaker. She raised their children. My grandparents were Isaac and Mary Elizabeth Miller. They had four children: three sons, Julius, Matthew (deceased) and David and one daughter Elizabeth Ann.

This was another God-fearing family who honored God and took the Word to heart, and they raised their family to do the same. They lived by the Scripture which states that we should honor thy father and thy mother; that thy days may be long upon the land which the Lord thy God giveth thee.

My Miller great-grandfather and grandfather were farmers and entrepreneurs.They worked hard to provide for their families.

I am elated to know the rich history of both sides of my family. They were families that loved God and their families. They had a great work ethic and a strong desire to make things better for the next generations. The families knew how to save their dollars and keep the money coming back to their communities. But most of all they had a strong sense of pride and were determined to make their own way in this world. It brings me joy to know that I am a part of the five generations stemming from these families and that our legacy of love continues.

Yes, I Found Hope and JOY Again

By Wendy Johnson

Yes, I Found Hope and JOY Again

By Wendy Johnson

There's a quote that says, "Children are a blessing from the Lord." Author unknown.

In the same year that we were married, we were expecting our first blessing from the Lord. Unfortunately, it was not to be as I had a miscarriage.

I remember screaming and praying upon seeing the light spotting, then the brownish discharge, and then the bright red blood clots! I questioned God, "Why Lord, I've been good. Don't you love me?" I immediately went to Him in prayer and I picked up my Bible. The Scripture that popped up in my focus was, "The Lord is close to the brokenhearted and saves those who are crushed in spirit. "Psalm 34:18

One day in 1982, I experienced bleeding followed by cramping and pain in my lower abdomen. I passed a large blood clot, the size of a lemon. This is my second miscarriage. It was at this point that I began to cry out to God seeking an understanding of what was wrong with me. I just didn't understand it. Why was this happening to me?

As time went on, we didn't give up! I refused to give up. We continued to try for our third blessing. Yes, I said "third" because we never forget our first two babies.

In 1983, we relocated to the Panama Canal and lived in a beautiful home on Fort Clayton Army Base. Shortly after arriving there, excitement was in the air! We found out that we were pregnant again. Now that I think about it, the word "excitement" is an understatement. My due date was one week after my birthday. What a very special birthday gift this would be!

As the day grew closer, preparing the nursery became my primary focus. I only had one more thing that needed to be done and that was to hang the curtains in this very special room. I was determined to hang them myself rather than wait for my husband to do it. Huge Mistake! I went into labor two days later.

Sadly, our baby choked on the umbilical cord, and I had a term stillborn on my birthday!

Again, I was devastated! The umbilical cord strangled my baby boy, cutting off his oxygen flow. It's called a nuchal cord, and it happens when a baby's umbilical cord is wrapped around his neck. I didn't get to hear my baby's cry. I am grateful that I was able to hold him in my arms and my husband and I were given time to say our goodbyes to our angel baby.

It hurt so bad, and we felt a wide range of emotions. We struggled with grief, anxiety, shock, isolation, suffering and numbness. I had nightmares. This was so traumatic for both of us. And yet I continued to believe that God was still working.

After this miscarriage, I fell into a slight depression. I gave up on trying to have more children. When I asked my doctor for birth control, he refused to prescribe it.

I was in so much emotional pain. I was so hurt, and I wondered why all of this had happened – I Had Lost Three Babies! Oh, how my heart ached.

Still, I managed to get by. After all, I was “Smiling Wendy”, the one who was always there for everybody else. As I look back, I probably could have won an Oscar for acting as if everything was fine when, deep down, I was very sad and extremely broken.

Calls home to my family in the States were so expensive that I could only make a few of them each month. And whenever I spoke with my family, I tried to sound strong so they would not worry. It was a very difficult façade to maintain, and it was emotionally draining. I endured this for the entire four years that we lived in Panama.

I was exercising regularly and, on the outside, I looked amazing. On the inside, however, I was anything but amazing. In fact, I felt like complete trash. Here I was, far away from home, surrounded by these army families who all had children except for us. Seeing families with children constantly reminded me of what I felt we were missing. Our friends kept asking us when we were going to have children. I played it off and told them that we loved to travel and were waiting to grow our family.

Eventually, my doctor suggested that I go to group therapy. I was suffering fromPost Traumatic Stress Disorder, a disorder in which a person has difficulty recovering after experiencing a terrifying event. I was in a therapy group with other individuals who had experienced a loss of some kind. There were those who had lost limbs, homes, even families. While we all had different reasons for being there, the one thing that bonded us together is that we were all feeling hopeless.

Those were some very tough times. My days were full of sadness and depression. My nights were filled with tears because I cried, cried and cried some more.

I know for sure that this scripture is true, "Weeping may endure for a night, but joy comes in the morning." Psalm 30:5

Finally, I went back to God. God is my Father. I talk to Him like He's my dad. But this time instead of asking Him why, I surrendered it all to Him. I read the entire Bible. I stood on His promises.

Eventually He brought me out of my depression. God provided peace for me to find hope and joy again. Thank you, Jesus! After two years I was healed from my depression.

Soon, I found a job calling Bingo at the Fort Amador Officers Club. I worked there three days a week and I loved it!

Most of the customers were older retirees. They loved me because I was loud, entertaining and respectful. Imagine me, "Outgoing Wendy," calling those numbers with my unique blend of kindness and pizzazz, it was something that only I could do. I brought joy and happiness into that room!

Four years later, our blessing would arrive. Hallelujah! God blessed us with a beautiful daughter on April Fools Day. However, that pregnancy was not without a lot of fear and anxiety. I prayed and talked to God a lot about the delivery day. When I was about to go into labor, I told the Lord, "It's all in your hands".

Today, seeing my daughter teaching elementary school children warms my heart so much. I am filled with gratitude. She is married to a wonderful man, so guess what? My husband also got the son that he always wanted.

This painful place in my life had become my birthing place, for God restored our joy with our beautiful baby girl. Just when we had given up hope, God brought a miracle of light into our darkness. And she has been lighting up our hearts ever since.

My JOY is Living in the Key of "C"

By Lois Larkins

My JOY is Living in the Key of "C"

By Lois Larkins

I began this story on July 6, 2024, filled with some very mixed feelings. I had just taken my Loved One (LO) to a respite care facility. Why? Because I needed a break. I was uncertain of how to get him to agree to go, but I took my support group leader's advice. I told my LO, "I'm going on a vacation and so are you." It sounded a little harsh, but it worked! I had no problem getting him to go or to stay, however when I picked him up ten days later, he told me he was mad at me the whole time he was there. He also told me that he stayed in his room during his entire time.

I feel badly at times that I did this; however, I realize that I must stay focused and recognize that if I do not take care of myself, I will be in no shape to be a caregiver for my LO or for anybody else.

Since my LO is a disabled veteran, my resources come from the Veterans Affair (VA). The VA is responsible for payment of veterans' benefits, medical care for veterans, and their memorial accommodations. (If you have to use your own private resources for this care, I suggest you start your research by going to homeinstead.com, a company that assists with providing safe and consistent care for your LO.)

After that day in July, I put this story away. Today, August 6, 2024, I'm coming back to it. As usual, I am listening to the news that is on the television. I hear Minnesota's forty-first governor, Tim Walz, say to the forty-ninth Vice President of the United States of America, Kamala

Harris, "Thank you for bringing the joy back." Joy is certainly in the air. God bless America. So, before I continue, I would like to present a Scripture for your edification and reflection.

> *"You love him even though you have never seen him. Though you do not see him now, you trust him; and you rejoice with a glorious, inexpressible joy. The reward for trusting him will be the salvation of your souls." (1 Peter 1:8–9 NLT)*

It has been a chaotic and challenging past four weeks, and this Scripture is one of my favorites. It helps to keep me focused.

This is my third participation in the *Living in the Key of Joy* anthology project. Each time I've always thought about the keys on the piano, and have wanted to write about them, but I didn't. I cannot let the idea go this time because recently I had a baby grand piano dismantled and removed from my home. Among other problems, it was out of tune and was just too expensive to restore.

As you may know, a standard piano keyboard has eighty-eight keys: fifty-two white and thirty-six black. Oh, this makes me think back to when I was a young teenager saying that "if you are white, you are right; if you are black, you better get back; if you are brown, then stick around; and, if you are yellow, you are mellow." Oh my, I digressed. Anyway, a standard piano keyboard offers a range of seven full octaves plus three additional notes. An octave is every twelve keys (seven white keys and five black keys). In this *Living in the Key of Joy, Volume V* anthology, I am living in the Key of C, and since the number 3 is my favorite number, I want to have a little fun and go just a little deeper.

Normally three octaves on the piano get the most use. These three are in the center of the keyboard. They are octaves 3, 4, and 5. Each octave has keys C, D, E, F, G, A, and B along with the five black flat and sharp keys. Octave 4 is in the middle of the piano. Its notes are medium in pitch, not too high nor too low. This is the octave I try to sing in. Notice I said "try" to sing in. Octave 3 is one octave below, and its notes are moderately low. Octave 5 is one octave above Octave 4, and its notes are moderately high. In any octave the white keys are for the tones of the C major scale, C, D, E, F, G, A, and B.

If you want to play in the key of C, just start on any of the "C keys" and stick with the white notes only, and you have it. These keys are referred to as natural notes. I took piano lessons for about three years while a teenager and although I researched this information, I already knew it. I just had to refresh my memory. As a young adult I played the piano in weddings and played saxophone in a jazz band. Back then I played well, but I cannot play at all now. As the saying goes, "If you don't use it, you'll lose it."

Getting back to the joy that I have, it is Biblical joy, a gift from God. It is something the world cannot give and the world cannot take away. Joy is one of the nine Fruit of the Spirit as listed in Galatians, Chapter 5, Verses 22-23. Joy is so important to me as it is an essential part of Christian life.

As I consider how I can maintain my joy while dealing with difficult emotions, I think of three "C" words and that brings me to the core of my story. For me, living in the "key of C", relates to making a Choice, being a Caregiver, and Depending upon Christ.

Making a CHOICE

I made a choice when I decided that I would become a caregiver for my LO. I just did not expect my choice to come to fruition so soon. Illness comes in its own time and on its own terms.

I have a T-shirt that I wear sometimes when I take my LO to his doctor's appointments at the Veterans Administration Hospital. It says, "Being a wife is a choice, being a Veteran's wife is an honor." I always get thumbs up every time I wear it. I try to be mindful to thank him for his service often. It cheers him up.

I am glad I made a choice to take care of my own emotional health when I placed my LO into a respite facility for a short while. I needed a rest.

Despite being warned of some of the challenges that come with being a caregiver, I intentionally made the choice to serve in that role. As James 1:2 encourages me, I do *"count it all joy"* when facing various trials, knowing that they produce endurance and strengthen my faith. I often find myself meditating on this Scripture because I often feel as though I am the housekeeper and an errand girl. Honestly, at times, it is difficult not to become angry. Nevertheless, I choose inexpressible joy over anger.

I also choose my battles and sometimes I choose not to try to reason with my LO. If he says it is 3:00 P.M. and it is really 11:00 A.M, I have learned to just agree and move on to the next conversation.

Being a CAREGIVER

A caregiver is described as a family member or paid helper who continually looks after a LO. Their LO could be a child or a sick, elderly, or disabled person. I am a caregiver who provides direct care to a sick, elderly, disabled LO who is dealing with Alzheimer's, dementia, and is prone to frequent falls. He also has a whole heap of other medical issues.

Caregivers often must deal with family conflicts; that's certainly been the case for me. Even though my LO's family deserted him 12 years ago, they have been responsible for multiple police visits to my home. In 2024 alone, police officers came to my house at least five times to conduct wellness checks, as they must follow-up on all complaints of elder abuse. I've also been visited by social service counselors who have come to investigate and, of course, they have never found anything improper. Still, I pray for my family, friends, and foes.

Being a caregiver can be physically demanding and emotionally taxing especially when your LO thinks you are the enemy. It can lead to burnout and a stressful way of life. This is why it is important to join a support group. Being in a support group can help mitigate most of the challenges you will face. I am telling you what I know, not what I have read. After all I have written to this point, I can tell you that I do not have any problems compared to the complaints and concerns I hear in my support group meetings.

I am not even going to elaborate on the caregiver's feelings of social isolation and the challenges of trying to take time out for your own personal wellbeing; or doing simple things, like window shopping. Much of my shopping these days is done online, and the items are delivered to my doorstep.

In spite of all that I've described, there are positive things that can come from being a caregiver. It gives you deep satisfaction and a sense of purpose. It also provides the opportunity to learn new skills, to become a master at time management and a pro at exercising patience. Patience is another one of the fruits listed that make up the Fruit of the Spirit in Galatians 5:22.

There is a prayer that many saints often pray for in church that goes like this, "Lord, thank you for waking me up this morning in my right mind and having the use of my limbs." OMG! It has a whole new meaning to me now.

Seeing your LO not functioning in their right mind, barely able to walk without aid, and sometimes struggling to get dressed is an awakening and makes you want to live each day as if it were your last. In other words, you gain a greater appreciation for life, especially if you knew the person before their current problems became so prevalent. All I can say is that watching a LO deteriorate and become mean and defiant is emotionally draining. However, one of my favorite quotes talks about when we are compassionate people, many times we must go where it hurts, sometimes we must be alongside the person dealing with the emotional pain. It truly shows we care. This means that not only are we sometimes broken, but also beaten up and beaten down when we see our LO hurting, fearful, or confused. This brings me to my final Key of C, Christ.

Depending on CHRIST

Because I trust Christ and depend on my relationship with Him, I was able to make the choice to be a caregiver. And, despite it all, I have Biblical joy, you know, the joy that the world did not give me and cannot take it away. The joy I have is not simply an emotion or a short-lived moment of happiness. This joy I have surpasses the temporary highs and lows of my life's journey. Another Scripture that gives me hope and keeps me focused is Romans 15:13 ESV where it says, "May the God of hope fill you with all joy and peace in believing, so that by the power of the Holy Spirit you may abound in hope."

The Biblical joy I have is rooted in my faith and I can only continue having it by keeping my trust in Him. "A joyful heart is good medicine, but a crushed spirit dries up the bones" (Proverbs 17:22 ESV). When I find myself getting a little lonely, tired or sad I remember another Scripture, Psalm 126:5 ESV, that says, "Those who sow in tears shall reap with shouts of joy!" And, of course, Psalm 30:5 ESV which says, Weeping may tarry for the night, but joy comes with the morning."

I want to leave you with three quotes by a Dutch Catholic priest, who was also a professor, writer, and theologian.

> *Joy does not simply happen to us. We must choose joy and keep choosing it every day.* ~ Henri Nouwen
>
> *The greatest gift you can give yourself is a little bit of your own attention.* ~ Henri Nouwen
>
> *Compassion asks us to go where it hurts, to enter into the places of pain, to share in brokenness, fear, confusion, and anguish.* ~ Henri Nouwen

As I end my story, I want to say something about one of the five heavenly crowns mentioned in the New Testament – The Crown of Rejoicing (a badge of royalty). The other four crowns are: The Imperishable Crown, The Crown of Righteousness, The Crown of Glory, and The Crown of Life. 1 Thessalonians 2:19 ESV talks about The Crown of Rejoicing. It says, "For what is our hope or joy or crown of boasting before our Lord Jesus at his coming? Is it not you?" Also, Revelation 21:4 tells us that The Crown of Rejoicing will be our reward where God will wipe away every tear and there will be no more death, nor sorrow, nor crying, nor pain. What a joy it is to think about receiving this reward one day.

My JOY is **J**ust **O**nly **Y**ashua. Without Him I can do nothing. So, you see, I was able to make the Choice to be a Caregiver because of Christ. I certainly can do all things through Him who strengthens me. One last thing: I am glad and filled with joy that I did not choose Him, but He chose me.

I Found JOY in a Tote Bag

Dr. Katrina E. Miller

I Found JOY in a Tote Bag

By Dr. Katrina E. Miller

If you know me well, you know that I love tote bags. I mean I *really* love tote bags. Some might even dare to say I am obsessed! It doesn't matter what size, what is printed on it, or what material the tote is made of. Tote bags and I have "a thing going on." For fear of judgment, I wouldn't dare tell you how many I have. Let's just say one Thanksgiving everyone who took home leftovers left with a tote bag to carry their goodies in. There were over 20 people at my house that year and yes, I still had tote bags left.

I am not sure when my love for tote bags began. It might have been when I was a little girl, and I learned that I could carry ALL my toys in one bag! I like purses and handbags also. Just like some women love shoes or jewelry, I love tote bags.

Adding to this tote bag fixation is the fact that I am a speech-language pathologist. To give you a little more context, let me explain. Most speech pathologists travel between several facilities or schools to provide therapy to their patients or students. Therefore, many speech pathologists' automobiles are loaded with therapy materials and folders.

I know when I first started my career, I assigned each building I visited a specific color. For example, Douglas Elementary was my "yellow school" and Tubman Middle School was my "green school." When I arrived at Douglas Elementary, I would grab my yellow tote bag, which had all the materials I needed to provide treatment to the students at that school. When I went to Tubman Middle, I would grab the green tote. See how these tote bags helped to keep me organized?

To add insult to injury, speech language pathologists have gotten the nickname "bag ladies" because we seem to always have more than one bag. Speech Pathology companies provide lots of "free" tote bags at our speech conventions. It is not unusual to see fellow speech pathologists at these conventions with several or, like me, armfuls of tote bags. One year a medical company had the neatest silver glitter tote bags. I talked the representative into sending me several boxes of these silver bags for my students. Free of charge!! Man, I love a tote bag.

So just where did the concept of a tote bag originate? Naturally, the academic in me went in search of the history of the tote bag. Here's the story:

The concept of a tote bag originated in 1944 from the L.L. Bean company. Folks needed a reliable way to transport ice blocks from the car to the freezer. Presto! A canvas water resistant bag was created. Folks soon realized that these durable tote bags were good not just for carrying ice but for other household chores as well, and soon thereafter they became a shopping accessory. Today, L.L. Bean's "Boat Bag" is their most popular tote bag and it is based on the original design of the ice bag.

Of course, all true handbag lovers have heard of the iconic Birkin Bag. In case you don't know, these bags are more than high end. A look at their website reveals that these handbags cost thousands of dollars. And those are the used ones! There is even a story that a few years ago a Birkin handbag sold for a quarter of a million dollars at an online Christie's auction. Anyway back to the story...

Jane Birkin, who was a British actress, singer and fashion genius, often traveled around town with a large oversized woven basket. She loved this basket because it was large enough to carry all her essentials. Naturally the fashion industry was horrified, but Jane didn't care. Although the material was inflexible, Jane continued to use her wicker basket to carry snacks for her daughters, flowers, etc. As the story goes, one day during an argument her husband deliberately drove over her favorite basket. Days later she was on a flight with Hermes` chief executive Jean-Louis Dumas. Her new replacement wicker basket slipped out of the overhead cabinet and items fell all over the cabin. Dumas offered to make Jane a new tote bag and the infamous "Birkin Bag" was born. Jane loved the "stripped-down" elegance of the tote bag, and it became the "must have" fashion item. For many millionaires, the Birkin bag is still a must-have fashion accessory.

The popularity of the tote bag soared in the 1980s. It was around this time that the Strand bookstore in New York introduced its own design for a simple tote bag. Their tote bag advertised the name of the store, which opened the floodgates for other independent and neighborhood shops to follow. Everyone wanted to advertise their businesses on fabric and paper tote bags.

Today, restaurants, department stores, and jewelry stores use paper tote bags for their merchandise. Not only do these bags provide a great way for you to bring your items home from these establishments, but they also provide a way for merchants to advertise their goods and services. And consumers love them, especially those who live in states and counties where they are charged for store bags.

Well, this newfound information has truly increased my love for tote bags. I have tote bags to help me remember places I have visited, memorable purchases, and just to carry my favorite items. I remember the faces of my graduate students when they received a silver tote bag to symbolize their movement to “graduation” status. I really should buy stock in a tote bag company.

I once saw a tote bag in a woman’s hatchback that was given away at one of our national speech conventions. I went up to the woman and asked her “Are you a speech pathologist?" Of course, she answered “Yes”. I then shared with her how I saw her tote bag in the hatchback. We had a great laugh and shared a little about our careers and professions. Even though this woman didn’t look like me, it was a great opportunity to see how we are more alike than different. This incident also demonstrates how a simple tote bag can make the world seem a little smaller.

Well, this story might not have convinced you to buy an extra tote bag or even fully explain my obsession with them. This one thing I do know is that when you now see an L.L. Bean canvas “boat” bag you will remember its origins and the original purpose. Also, if you are ever close enough to see a Birkin handbag you will remember Jane and her love for wicker baskets. Not to mention how her husband ran over her favorite wicker basket. Finally, I would even dare to say when you see that next tote bag (and trust me you will see one) you just might think of this author and how she has found joy, so much joy, in a tote bag.

History retrieved (8/24/24) from: https://hozencollection.com/blogs/hozen-blog/history-of-tote-bag

The JOY of Chess

By Mariah Miller

The JOY of Chess

By Mariah Miller

Introduction

I wanted to create a poem that would encourage others and remind them of just how much Jesus loves us. I wanted the poem to acknowledge that we are free to embrace Joy as we are divinely guided by His Holy Spirit.

The poem I wrote and am sharing with you was inspired by Jesse Miller Jr, my father, and it's based on some of our conversations and the encouragement he has given to me. His exact words, "Life is like a game, so get in it!" have been a guiding force in my life.

I hope you'll use this poem as visual art and that it allows you to metaphorically see the correlation between God's love and a game of chess. In chess there are many things going on. Sometimes you need to move and think quickly, while at other times you need to just wait and see how things play out. These slower times are very much like how sometimes we need to be still and wait for God's instructions. As believers of Christ, we may endure many challenges as we stand in faith, but the Lord has both our back and our front.

At times I've felt very disappointed by God, very angry with God, and I chose to be stagnant. I was not happy about being labeled an unmarried single mother, felt like I was just barely making it, and then had to deal with discovering that I am neurodivergent. It wasn't until I started to move a little differently, study God's word more frequently, forgive and repent that I could see and understand that Joy comes from the journey, for it is our story.

I am grateful to have a wonderful daughter to care for, a chance to be made wiser and to rediscover myself in Christ. This makes me think of Philippians 4:11- 13 – "Not that I speak in regard to need, for I have learned that whatever state I am in, to be content: I know how to be abased, and I know how to be abound. Everywhere and in all things, I have learned both to be full and to be hungry, both to abound and suffer need. I can do all things through Christ that strengthens me."

Chess teaches us that we must have many different strategies and the same is true with life. We need a Plan A, Plan B and a Plan C. Even though our walk as believers may come with difficulties, Joy is available to us. Joy comes from knowing God's character and knowing that He loves us. God brings victory, even in spite of our own bad moves and decisions. But how would you know? Well-known chess player Jose Raul Capablanca once said "A book cannot by itself teach how to play, it can only serve as a guide, and the next must be learned by experience".

My goals are to stay the course, trust in Christ, and always remember that God is always in control, regardless of what it looks like.

The JOY of Chess

We are like chess pieces in God's plan
His chosen instruments, selected and divinely orchestrated
Marching into the new, toward the truth and the life, under the covenant keeper.
Accepting the invitation to be drafted into His army to fight for the king and His kingdom
Prepared for a battle, with each piece at will

Everything created to move in the way it was created
Who will win in the chess game of salvation?

Like a pawn taking one step of faith at a time
Or a rook that holds much influence
Cunning and strategic as a bishop,
Maneuvering impulsively and unpredictably as a knight
Divinely protected as a queen, basking in his favor for there is much value to the king.

The black and white squares set the stage, representing our choices and decisions
Planted in the wilderness, but we are not lost
The enemy's nature is murderous, he's the criminal of theft and sabotage
By way of aggressive tactics and cunning schemes
The enemy aims to bait, scoff and destroy our dreams
But what is fear when we have love?
Only considering the heart and the things above

The Grandmaster, the eye who sees the whole board,
Charges us to be wise as serpents, innocent as doves, like our Lord
As we walk in the spirit, He will instruct and teach us
We have been gifted to bring order and hope
Considering not our own limitations, but focused only on His irresistible grace
And never placing oneself in a box for there will be no space

The master strategist will order our steps
We have a perspective that is as the mind of Christ
Faith and Belief that resides in our hearts
We have gratitude for purpose as a free man

Wisdom is something that only the world can't seem to comprehend,
The Lord orders our steps, no move for human nature to play
As we learn to master our passions and patience, we find victory
Strength and faith as keys, as we move in faith
From the first move to the last, this is how precisely He cares for us
All the while using our enemies as tools for His greater purpose
To educate, strengthen and grow in our faith.
To be called holy, favored and blameless
Clothed with a humble heart and clean hands
We are as good soldiers who suffer for Christ

Recollecting that the world and its evil desires will surely pass away
Our enemies of darkness shall be taken down
There's darkness and then there's light,
Created all by good, it's only a fixed fight

You see, the word of God and people are only forever (Eternal)
Ending with our enemy defeated by fire
And we are crowned as righteous
For God's love is sacrificial, God's character is loyal
He provides righteousness and justice to his precious believers
And it is our faith in God that has got us far
Embraced by His love, feels like the joy of chess.

I've Found JOY
In Lifetime Friendships

By Betty W. Temple

I've Found JOY
In Lifetime Friendships

By Betty W. Temple

Hi, my name is Betty, and I want to share with you one of the areas in my life that gives me joy. But first, let me tell you a little about myself…

I was born in the small city of Portsmouth, Virginia. I lived there with my parents and six siblings. I was the fifth child born to my parents, I had four brothers and two sisters.

I grew up during the time of segregation, though it impacted my older siblings more than it impacted the younger ones of us. My mother was extremely protective of us because she knew the stories of slavery and had experienced the pains of segregation.

There was a store in our city called Grant. It sold a variety of things, including household goods, hair products, and toys. There was an area in this store where food was prepared by a short order cook.

If my mother or I got hungry, we could purchase food there, but we had to take our food out of the store to enjoy it. The manager did not allow Black people to eat at the table or the counter in that store. During that time, I was young and did not realize what was taking place.

To protect my innocence my mother always made things a game. She would do things or say things like, "Let's go to the bus stop and while we are there let's count the cars that go by." Or she would have me read the street signs. She did what she could to try to distract me from noticing how badly we were being treated by the White people around us.

Eventually the time came for me to start elementary school and that's where I began to experience the particular joy I want to tell you about.

In the first grade I met two girls, Joyce and Beverly, and we became friends. We all lived in the same community.

As time went by, I met another girl in the community who lived next door to Beverly. We called her Sissy, and she became one of our close friends.

When Joyce, Beverly, and I went to middle school, a new girl moved into the community. Her name was Francis, and she also became a good friend.

The four of us went to public school and Sissy went to a Catholic school. It wasn't until high school that the five of us were together in the same school. We attended the famous I.C. Norcom High School. This was the only high school Black children could attend at that time.

We did not have bus transportation to school, so we walked. There were about 20 or 25 students in our group, taking the hike to school. We walked regardless of the weather.

The girls had a dress code to abide by during those days. We could not wear pants in school; however, if there was harsh weather, we could wear them *to* school and then put them in our lockers until it was time to walk home.

We had a wonderful time in high school. We went to games, pep rallies, dances, proms, other activities, and we had boyfriends. We totally enjoyed that time of our lives.

One memory that we can now laugh about is walking to school and having to cross the train track. Once we reached a certain point, we would run into the children who lived in the project housing development in that area. They charged a quarter to anyone who needed to cross the train track to get to school. If you didn't pay it, there would be a problem, regardless of your gender.

But Joyce, Beverly, Francis, Sissy, and I never had to pay to cross the track. That's because the boys who lived in the project housing knew us and knew our brothers. These boys watched over us like sisters.

For example, they made it clear to us that if they were planning to start something they would give us one warning. And they made sure we understood that if we didn't heed that one warning, it was our own fault.

On one occasion we were at a football game against Booker T. Washington High School. Booker T. was our rival school. We received our one warning and we paid attention. We swiftly left the game. By the time we got to the bus stop, we heard gunfire.

There was another occasion when we were at a pool party in another community. We were trying to get our last dance in when we got our warning. Again, we quickly left the premises. My friends and I had just made it out of the gate when the project guys tossed a Molotov cocktail across the fence.

We loved to dance and went dancing often, even in different cities. We would dance until we were sweaty. We often went to Beverly's parents' home to turn records and dance. We had a wonderful time no matter where we went.

One time Beverly and I went on a double date. We had never experienced what I'm going to share with you.

I dated a guy named Paul at that time and his best friend was Poochie. They were students at Crestwood High School in Chesapeake, Virginia. Paul and Poochie invited Beverly and I out for an evening of dinner and dancing. We accepted.

Before we could leave, the car we were in had a flat tire. Paul and Poochie took the tire off of a neighbor's car and placed it on the car they were going to drive. They had a name for the vehicle they drove, it was "The Iron Horse." Beverly and I quickly learned why it had that name. In order to keep the driver's door closed Beverly had to put her arm around Poochie and hold the door.

The car had a stick shift and Poochie had to use a wrench to shift gears. Not only that, but the car also had a heater that discharged hot water. Can you imagine how dangerous that was? The back seat of the vehicle was very neat. However, the neatness of the car was due to the hole in the floor. Anyone seated in the back could dispose of their garbage through that hole.

We really enjoyed our time with the guys and laughed often. By the way, Paul and Poochie replaced the tire on the neighbor's car when they returned home.

In our community there was not only a church and an elementary school, but also a grocery store, an ice cream store, and a pharmacy. This pharmacy had an area where we could order and purchase food. One day my friends and I went there to get something to eat. We waited for our turn to place our orders, however the worker kept overlooking us as she waited on the White customers. We finally got tired of standing and sat in one of the booths. The worker hurried to wait on us then because we had just staged a sit-in.

Joyce, Beverly, Francis, and I were regularly active in our church. We attended Sunday service, Sunday School, weekly Bible Study, and we sang in the choir. Mrs. Harmon was the choir director at that time. When she needed someone to fill in for a tenor or an alto she would use me. To this day, because I sang soprano, alto, and tenor, I sing all three parts in one song. I never stay in one key!

I taught Vacation Bible School two summers in my home church. I enjoyed attending Vacation Bible School so much that I often attended programs in two additional churches.

After graduating high school we all went to college. Joyce, Beverly, Francis, and I entered Norfolk State College, now known as Norfolk State University. Sissy left the area and attended North Carolina A&T.

During our college days we saw, met and dated handsome young men! Sometimes we all dated together and even gathered at Beverly's parents' home on occasion. This was when we found out how fathers could make us laugh when joking about our boyfriends' appearances. Now remember, this was the time of afros and miniskirts.

One time Beverly's dad was joking about the boy Francis dated. He said, "You have some pretty white teeth, that's because you are so black." We laughed so hard, and no one was upset, because we understood how our fathers could behave.

My dad had his comments, as well. One day I was on my way to Norfolk State, and I was wearing a mini skirt and, of course, Dad had something to say. His comment was, “What do you have on, a wide belt?” I broke out laughing.

There was another time when my dad had me laughing. My fine boyfriend came to see me, sporting his big afro. Dad answered the door, and came to me saying, “Betty, that boy with the mop on his head is here to see you.” Here I go, laughing again.

Beverly and Francis left college after their first semester. Francis went to New York to work, and Beverly went to work in Washington, DC. I didn’t want Beverly to leave the area and threatened to destroy her application for a job to work at the FBI. I finally gave her the application and off she went.

Joyce and I graduated from Norfolk State and started our careers. Years later we all got married and had children.

Joyce was the first one to marry and we all participated in her wedding party. This was the first time any of us had been in a wedding.

As time and life went on, things occurred. Joyce and Sissy lost their spouses at an early age. Joyce’s husband Sam was the first Black Police Officer to drive a motorcycle in Portsmouth.

Beverly and Francis are still married. Francis and Ernest have been married 44 years. Beverly and Ken have been married 51 Years. As for me, I’ve been divorced 43 years, not counting my separation.

Through it all, we always stayed in contact with each other and even checked on each other’s parents.

Six years ago, I invited these friends to join me in celebrating our 70th birthdays in Las Vegas. Sissy lives in that area and we were all gathered there for a week. It was an amazing time together. We enjoyed shows, movies, the Grand Canyon, the spa, sightseeing, eating out at different restaurants, and of course shopping.

Even now we occasionally come together, and we totally enjoy each other. It is as if no time has passed, and we just pick up from where we left off.

This year we all will be turning 76 years old. We still stay connected even though we live in different states and cities. Joyce lives in Maryland, Beverly lives in Georgia, Sissy in Nevada, Francis and I live in different parts of Virginia.

In my life, good friends have been crucial and these friends of over 70 years are an amazing fellowship of supporters. We speak the truth to each other, show love, faith, and compassion. We uplift one another and even now at this age, we continue to grow together. And we come together if there is a need.

Anytime you have a true friendship from childhood through adulthood, God has truly blessed you.

I give thanks to God for aligning me with these amazing women who are encouragers and my dear, true friends. God knew what and who I needed. I am totally a blessed woman full of joy for the "lifetime women" in my life.

The JOY of Speaking Words of Life

Yolanda Fields-Witherspoon

The JOY of Speaking Words of Life

Yolanda Fields-Witherspoon

"Sticks and stones may break my bones, but words can never hurt me." I've heard this familiar expression for years, but really didn't think much about it. It wasn't until I became a seasoned Christian that I realized how much weight it held. That expression is not true, it's a lie. Words really do hurt and, in some instances, they can scar people for life. I know this from personal experience. I've heard the negative words people have said about me -- to my face hurt and behind my back – and some of them prevented me from accomplishing the things I wanted to achieve. On the other hand, some of that negative talk just made me more determined to prove people wrong and to reach my goals.

Over the years, I've heard words of defeat from teachers, professors, classmates, relatives, bosses, employees, boyfriends, and from people I thought were my friends. I heard words like, "You are ugly", "You will never go to college", "Don't ask that dumb question in class", "You'll never graduate", "You are not smart enough to be a speech-language pathologist, you need to change your major.", "You need to prove yourself", "You'll never lose the weight", "You get fatter every time I see you" "You are not intelligent enough for me", "You don't stimulate me with your intellect" "I didn't say that I wanted to see you", "I don't want you. I'm sick and tired of this."

I even heard words of defeat swirling around in my own head as I directed defeating thoughts and words toward myself. I've heard myself say to myself, "I'll never lose this weight" "Will I ever be successful?" "Will I ever overcome this battle?".

Yes, these were certainly words that hurt and attempted to defeat me. They were designed to hinder the blessings and plans God had for me from the foundation of the earth. Thankfully, I didn't allow them to consume me, I trusted that God always had a remnant for me. He always had people in my life who spoke life to me and provided words to inspire and encourage me.

The first, and most important, people who spoke life to me were my parents, Floyd and Barbara Fields. Whenever I was given a crushing blow, they would always counteract that blow with words of life, strength, encouragement and a great deal of unconditional love. They spoke words such as, "I know you can do this!" "You can do all things through Christ that strengthens you", "You are beautiful" "You are smart." "They can't take away what you have learned." "You are going to make it!" "I'm so proud of you."

Others in my life have also provided words of encouragement as well as prophesied such things as, "You are headed for greatness" "You always have a word of encouragement for me" "You are a blessing to me" "You light up the entire room" You brought back laughter into our home" "You rock my world" "You made my day" "You make me smile" "You bring me joy!"

When I think about how words have been used to hurt and to help me, I must say that the old saying I started with really does carry a great deal of weight.

Research has shown how words, whether negative or positive, can have a very profound affect over our lives. Here are just a few examples:

"Negative effects of negative self-talk, 1) increases stress and anxiety, 2) lowers self-esteem, 3) opens the door for symptoms of depression and 4) creates self-sabotage. On the other hand, positive effects of positive self-talk, 1) increases confidence and self-esteem, 2) improves mood and resilience, 3) increases better decision making and 4) enhances performance." (Search Labs/AI Overview, September 2024).

Ultimately, research shows that "the way people speak to themselves can significantly impact their mental health, self-esteem, confidence and even their relationships with others. Positive self-talk often leads to improved mood and performance, while negative self-talk can lead to stress, anxiety and depression. One of the best weapons against negative self-talk is being kind to yourself by 1) identifying negative patterns, 2) using affirmations, 3) focusing on accomplishments and 4) practicing self-compassion." (Search Labs/AI Overview, September 2024).

In Proverbs 18:21 it reads, "Death and life are in the power of the tongue, and those who love it and indulge it will eat its fruit and bear the consequences of their words" (Amplified Bible). This is a Scripture that many of us have heard for years, but I must say that as I have become more seasoned in life it carries a great deal more weight and substance for me. In Genesis chapter one, we read that God spoke twelve times and what He spoke came to pass. He spoke words of faith which resulted in life; not words of defeat which would have led to defeat.

According to Charles Capps, "Words are the most powerful things in the universe. Words are containers. They carry faith, or fear, and they produce after their kind." Charles Capps further shares in his book entitled, "God's Creative Power" that God revealed to him that, "People can have what they say but they are saying what they have."

We must diligently practice saying the right words to ourselves and our situations. We must speak life and not defeat. We must speak those things that are not as though they are, , as mentioned in Romans 4:17. We must understand that as we speak the right words into our lives and situations that our faith is strengthened. Romans 10:17 states, "So faith comes from hearing (what is told), and what is heard comes by the preaching of the message concerning Christ" (Amplified Bible).

Joel Osteen, in his book entitled, "Speak the Blessing: Send Your Words in the Direction You Want Your Life to Go" states, "Are you going to give life to defeat and doubt and talk about how you'll never get well or are you going to release the miracle?" This can apply to every area of our lives. Are we going to give life to defeat and doubt by talking about how we'll never accomplish our goals, never lose weight, never get out of debt, never get married, never finish school, or never overcome the addictions in our lives? Or are we going to release the miracles intended for our lives by speaking those things that are not as though they were? We can overcome every situation as we put faith to our words and as we speak the word of God to every situation in our lives. As Charles Capps stated, "The word of God conceived in the heart, formed by the tongue, and spoken out of the mouth is creative power."

When I reflect on my own life, there have been many times when I had to stop and learn to speak life into my situation. I recall the time when I was studying for my boards to become certified as a Speech-Language Pathologist and the enemy was speaking a lot of negative words in my head, words designed to defeat me. I recognized some of these as words I'd heard in my past and here they were again. Things like, "You are not going to pass this test", "You are not smart enough", "You won't be able to finish it in time", "What makes you think you are ready to take this test and pass it?", "Forget about it, you were already told that you are not good enough to be a speech-language pathologist!", "You need to move on to something else." Oh, my goodness, boy did I have to fight! The week before I had to take the Boards I was traveling home from Washington DC with these negative thoughts plaguing my mind. But that's when I spoke life to the situation. I fought back with the Word of God and I told myself, "I can do all things through Christ that strengthens me", "I am smart", "I do have what it takes", "God knows the plans what He has for me, plans to prosper me and not to harm me", "I am a winner", "I am going to pass this test!" Oh yes, by the time I finished encouraging myself I felt like Wonder Woman! This test was NOT going to defeat me, I was determined to defeat it!!

On the day of the exam, while those old negative thoughts were trying to invade my mind once again, I said, "Devil you are a liar, I do have the victory today! "I cast down imaginations and every high thing that exalt itself against the knowledge of God and bring into captivity every thought unto the obedience of Christ", II Corinthians 10:5 (King James Version). Once I said those overcoming words, all of those defeating thoughts vanished! I finished the test on time and, praise God, I passed the test, both literally and spiritually.

We must learn to speak positive, affirming words to ourselves, despite what things look like, feel like, or seem like. The Word of the Lord says, "Trust in and rely confidently on the Lord with all your heart and do not rely on your own insight or understanding. In all your ways know and acknowledge and recognize Him, and He will make your paths straight and smooth (removing obstacles that block your way)" Proverbs 3:5-6 (Amplified Bible).

While my husband and I were living in Beavercreek, Ohio he called me one day very much in a panic because he thought that he'd left his wallet at a gas station. He checked the gas station, but it wasn't there. I then asked him to check at Walmart since he had gone there as well. Just thinking about the size of this store, I had every reason to doubt that he'd find it there. So, of course, this was a perfect time for those old negative thoughts to raise their ugly heads again. We both heard things like, "You know somebody has already found the wallet and they have taken all the money and credit cards.", "You will never find that wallet.", "What are you going to do if you don't find it, you have to pay your bills!", "Your credit is ruined; someone now has access to all of your accounts!" My husband was also worried about how he was going to take care of his home without his money. Pure fear and panic attempted to flood our very being at that moment, however righteous indignation rose up in me and I began to speak the word of God to the situation.

"We thank you Lord for the victory in Christ Jesus. We thank you Lord that we are tithers and you rebuke the devourer for our sakes. We thank you that no weapon formed against us shall prosper. I plead the blood over my husband's wallet, and we thank you that everything is in his wallet and it is untouched in the name of Jesus. We thank you that you are restoring that wallet to us in Jesus' name. You said in your Word, Lord, that if we speak your word in faith nothing wavering, we can have whatsoever we say. Your Word cannot return to you void when we speak in faith therefore, we thank you in advance for the wallet to be restored to us intact in Jesus' name!"

By the time we finished praying there was a sense of calm. We just believed what we said in faith.

My husband went to Walmart and, shortly after we had spoken, he called me back to report that someone had turned in the wallet and EVERYTHING was intact! Hallelujah!! The power of speaking life to your situation, despite what it looks like, is real and this story illustrates what it can look like.

Lastly, through life's challenges, I learned, and it's become a rhema word to me, that death and life is in the power of the tongue. As a result of this becoming a rhema word, here are a few affirmations I speak daily:

I Can Do It, Nothing to It!
I am a winner.
I am the best of the best.
I'm a champion.
I believe in myself.
I think positive thoughts.
I am focused.
I love myself.
My attitude determines my altitude in life.
I have no fear of rejection.
I do not have the spirit of fear but of love, power and a sound mind.
I am disciplined.
I am healthy.
I am successful.
I am determined.
I am organized.
I am smart.
I am intelligent.
I am a giver.
I make great decisions.
I attract the right people to me.
I am more than a conqueror.
I am victorious.
I am loved.
I am on my way to the top!
I love to read.
I love to learn.
I will always do my best.

I am confident.
I am special.
I have what it takes.
I can do whatever I need to do in life.
I can do all things through Christ that strengthens me.
I choose divine health.
I choose life today.
I will make good decisions for my body this year.
I choose health this year.
I wish above all that I prosper and be in health even as my soul prospers.
I am a piece in a very big picture, the picture that will change the world for God's glory.
I am a dynamic member of the body of Christ.

As I close, I'd like to share two important points that Charles Capps suggests are important to speaking the right words into your life: Point One: "The word of God conceived in the heart, formed by the tongue, and spoken out of the mouth is creative power." Point Two: "Jesus said, "I have told my people they can have what they say," but "My people are saying what they have."

Yes, indeed I have learned and continue to learn the importance of speaking the right words into my life. Doing so has afforded me the joy I experience in my spiritual, personal and professional life.

References

Amplified Bible
Capps, Charles. *God's Creative Power: Will Work for You.* Capps Publishing, 1976.
Capps, Charles. *God's Creative Power for Healing.* Capps Publishing, 1991.
*King James Version Bible

Osteen, Joel. *Speak the Blessing: Send Your Words in the Direction You Want Your Life to Go.* Hachette Book Group, Inc., 2024.
Psychology Today. *How to Quiet Our Negative Self-Talk.* PsychologyToday.com, May 11, 2024.
Search Labs/AI Overview, September 2024.

MEET THE PRESENTER
GAIL CLANTON

As a professional writing coach, Gail hosts writing workshops designed to help adults embrace the value of their stories. Various themes are used as students learn to more fully recognize the power of their words and how to use them as they reflect, rejuvenate, educate, and encourage. Several of these stories have been included in anthologies, as well as solo book projects, published through Clanton Communications LLC. As a speaker, Gail shares with groups of all sizes on topics ranging from the personal to the professional. She's spoken about her personal life experiences (divorce, disappointment, and her amazing bounce back) and also shares her marketing and writing expertise from the stage.

A certified professional life coach, as well as a Christian life coach, Gail has a unique way of guiding and encouraging her clients toward their full potential. It's quickly obvious that she cares and wants them to succeed.

Her writing, as well as her coaching and speaking, are each sprinkled with a healthy dose of humor, honesty, and common sense. You'll leave her presence inspired to reach a higher level of joy and success, believing that you deserve nothing less.

Gail is the author of the Amazon best seller, *Sparkle In The Rain*, and her work has also appeared in two volumes of *The Black Woman's Book of Travel and Adventure, Our Fathers Which Art In Heaven,* and *Women Inspiring Nations*. This is her fifth anthology project (with more to come) and she is proud of having provided over 30 adults with a collaborative opportunity to share their stories.

When Gail isn't writing, coaching, or speaking, she enjoys singing, shopping, and traveling.

www.gailclanton.com
gail@gailclanton.com
Facebook: gailclantonsparkles
IG:gailclantonsparkles

MEET THE AUTHORS

SELECE W. BOWMAN

Selece W. Bowman is a Speech Language Pathologist and the Owner/Founder of Speak With Boldness, LLC. She has over 37 years of experience. Selece is a Howard University alumna.

She is excited to be a part of the *Living in the Key of Joy* project for the third time and hopes to encourage others through her story.

She enjoys reading, writing, singing, fishing, baking, playing Scrabble and praying with and for others.

She was born and raised in Washington, DC. She currently resides in Chesapeake, VA with her family. She attends New Life Church in Virginia Beach, VA.

DR. JAMIE J. BROWN

Dr. Jamie J. Brown embodies a remarkable fusion of resilience, advocacy, and empowerment. As a hard-of-hearing individual and an advocate for the Deaf community, she has over three decades of experience working with individuals in both the deaf and hearing communities. She is also a certified professional life coach.

She is also a recipient of the prestigious Presidential Lifetime Achievement Award and an Honorary Doctorate degree in Humanities.

Dr. Brown is a mentor fluent in American Sign Language, guiding students to develop confidence and proficiency in effective communication. Her commitment is driven by her mission to bridge the gap between the deaf and hearing worlds.

www.jamiejbrown.com

GEORGE D. CLANTON

George D. Clanton is a proud family man. He and his wife have raised three wonderful children – all of whom are now successful adults.

He likes being outdoors and especially enjoys biking, walking, and working in his yard. He's employed with the federal government as an IT Program Manager and is also deeply involved in the music ministry at his church.

George is excited to be a part of the *Living In The Key of Joy* project because it has given him a creative outlet – a way to express thoughts and feelings that he hopes will be a blessing to all who read his story.

DR. GENEVIEVE CROMER

Dr. Genevieve Cromer has dedicated 30 years to education, as she's inspired countless students in her classrooms and beyond. This schoolteacher is also a passionate community servant who actively contributes to her church and local initiatives. She is a proud mother of four wonderful sons and grandmother of six.

Dr. Cromer loves line dancing, traveling—especially cruising—and staying fit through walking. Born and raised in Washington, DC, she pursued her college education in Boston, MA, before returning to DC after 20 years in the Boston area. Her guiding principle is encapsulated in her favorite quote by Dr. Martin Luther King Jr.: "Unconditional love will have the final word in reality."

VALERIA ELLIOTT

Valeria Elliott is better known as Ms. V The Storyteller. She lost her voice at the age of six and didn't get it back until she was twenty-three years old. She started sharing personal stories with friends and co-workers and decided to turn them into a podcast.

Ms. V is a speaker, coach, and author who believes that stories have the potential to educate, heal, free, and propel people into making new and better choices. As such, she now uses her gift of storytelling to help entrepreneurs find, write, and tell their fingerprint stories for business and branding.

MAURICE FOUSHEE

Maurice Foushee appreciates his retired federal employee status. He contributed to volumes II and III of *Living in the Key of Joy* and has written articles for his local chapter of his hobby. He occasionally wrote short limericks or rhymes for some co-workers.

He has been actively involved in several organizations by serving in leadership and supportive roles. His current affiliations or memberships include Queen's Chapel United Methodist Church; Alpha Phi Alpha Fraternity, Incorporated; Howard D. Woodson Senior High School Alumni Association; Washington Numismatic Society; Hillcrest Community Civic Association; and American Association of Geographers.

Maurice enjoys swimming, bowling, walking, numismatics (coin and banknote collecting), reading about finance and economics, and some yard work.

HEATHER HAMMOND

Heather Hammond is a native of Washington DC. She holds a Bachelor's Degree in Nursing from Howard University and a Master's Degree in Organizational Management in Public Health from Trinity University. She is a member of the Chi Eta Phi Sorority.

Heather enjoys spending time with her beautiful daughter, traveling, watching reality TV, going to plays and concerts, and listening to a variety of genres of music. She is a history buff, culinary enthusiast, and enjoys photography. Some of her favorite places to visit are beaches, parks, waterfront areas, and restaurants with great views. She sees the beauty of God in nature there. A constant learner, Heather believes we are never too old to learn new things.

IRMA D. HINTON

Irma Hinton is a proud native Washingtonian currently residing in Maryland. She is employed with the Federal Government and has over 35 years of civilian government service and experience. She is also a retired US Army veteran, who proudly served her country for 23 years before retiring in 2005.

Irma holds leadership positions in several clubs and organizations within her community, as well as with the military. Irma enjoys exercising, line dancing, traveling around the country and the world, planning social events and spending quality time with family and friends.

MAGDALENE JOHNSON

Magdalene Johnson has lived in the state of Maryland all of her life. She is currently a Senior Budget Analyst in Washington, DC and is looking forward to retiring soon. She earned both her undergraduate and graduate degrees from the University of Maryland in College Park.

Magdalene is active in her community civic association and other clubs and activities. She is a big fan of black and white films and has collected the entire original American Film Institute's (AFI) list of the 100 greatest movies ever. She's also a fan of Turner Classics Movies and is a lover of all animals.

MARIA MILLER JOHNSON

Maria Miller Johnson is a dedicated social worker, therapist, life coach, author and friend. Maria provides a listening ear, compassion and care to those facing life's challenges. She helps you to "Face It to Fit It" through, Belief, Courage, Enthusiasm and Commitment.

Maria has 30+ years of social work & community experience.

- Social Worker Anne Arundel County Public Schools in Annapolis, Maryland
- Therapist Awesome Thoughts Greenbelt, MD.
- Coach Miller Johnson with Dr. Lonise P. Bias Women of Light Speaker
- Worships Life Covenant Christian Ministries Accokeek, Maryland.

Maria and her husband Donald reside in Maryland with their four children and two grandchildren.

WENDY JOHNSON

Wendy Johnson is an "energetic, pearls-wearing, pompoms-carrying" Motivational Speaker, Certified Christian Life Coach and Author of "On A Positive Note".

As a Speaker and Coach, she captivates audiences with her positive messages to help them emerge from a negative mindset and reprogram mindsets one positive thought at a time. She is known as the "Positivity Professor." For the past 3 years, weekly, she has delivered a Facebook live, "Wake up with Wendy!"

Johnson has been married for 42 years to her husband, Sterling, and is the proud mom of one daughter, Jessica, who is a 4th grade schoolteacher.

Her memberships include the Red Hats Society, African Violets Book Club, and Hospitality Ministry Lead at The New Macedonia Baptist Church, Washington, DC.

LOIS LARKINS

Lois Larkins is an ordained minister and evangelist of the Gospel of Jesus. She has held ministry positions as Church Administrator, Director of Communications, Editor of New Members Manual, Bible Study teacher and other ministries. Currently, she is Executive Minister for Heart Changers Baptist Church in Silver Spring, Maryland. She oversees her own ministry, Inspired Minds on God (I.M.O.G. Networks Ministries, Inc).

Ms. Larkins' secular livelihood necessitated her being a Legal Secretary for prestige law firms in Washington DC/Miami FL, Network Administrator, Network Engineer, and Software Trainer.

Lois has a B.S. in Theology, The Sure Foundation Theological Institute, and is proud of her PHD (Praising Him Daily).

She can be contacted by Email: Lowrites3@gmail.com, LinkedIn: Lois Larkins, IG: Loislarkins111, and X (formerly Twitter): @Lslarkins.

LOISLARKINS.COM

DR. KATRINA E. MILLER

Dr. Katrina E. Miller is a Speech Language Pathologist and University Administrator in Northern Virginia. Dr. Miller has written professional articles and several textbook chapters including *Supervision the Other Side of Cultural Diversity* in Case Studies on Communication Disorders in Culturally Diverse Populations.

Dr. Miller recently published a book of devotionals entitled *SOAP Notes: Cleansing Thoughts for Healthcare Workers.* These devotionals were inspired by her day-to-day experiences as a Speech Pathologist.

Dr. Miller has enjoyed being a part of the *Living in the Key of Joy* anthology projects because they have not only allowed her to interact with new people, but to also share some of her life stories and experiences.

MARIAH MILLER

Mariah Miller is a daughter of the most high God and a mother of one. She enjoys serving her community. Mariah is a member of "Women of Light" organization founded by Dr. Lonise Bias.

Within her local church, she serves as an assistant teacher for Children's Church and an usher. She also serves as an event planner within the Living In Truth (L.I.T.) ministry at her church. L.I.T. provides support and guidance for the youth.

For six years, Mariah has served veterans and their families within the federal government workforce. She is so excited to be a part of this collection and is glad that she gave a big "YES" when the invitation was extended. She hopes her story will encourage those who read it.

BETTY W. TEMPLE

Betty W. Temple is the CEO of P.R.I.E.S.T. International Ministries. She believes in utilizing her gifts, walking in her calling, investing in the lives of others, and contributing to the Body of Christ.

In 2006 she accepted the call to the ministry and began her ministerial training. She received her ministerial license in 2008 and was ordained an Elder in 2009.

Elder Temple is known as a woman of prayer and often called "Prayer Warrior" and "General." She hosts weekly and monthly prayer calls on Zoom and offers educational Bible classes at various intervals.

YOLANDA FIELDS-WITHERSPOON

Yolanda Fields-Witherspoon works in the field of Speech Language Pathology and has expertise in the areas of management, entrepreneurship, clinical practice, and supervision. She has conducted numerous seminars and workshops on the local, state, and international levels. Yolanda serves on the board of several organizations revolving around the health disparities in this country and abroad.

Yolanda has participated in all of the volumes of *Living in the Key of Joy* and is excited about being a part of this last edition. She hopes her stories have ministered encouragement, love and inspiration.

Yolanda's hobbies include creating greeting cards, drawing, event planning, and spending time with family and friends.

Made in the USA
Middletown, DE
08 December 2024

66386071R00102